Salsas,

Sambals,

Chutneys

&

Chowchows

ALSO BY

CHRIS SCHLESINGER

AND

JOHN WILLOUGHBY

THE THRILL

OF THE GRILL

(1990)

SALSAS, SAMBALS, CHUTNEYS & CHOWCHOWS

CHRIS SCHLESINGER & JOHN WILLOUGHBY

PHOTOGRAPHY BY JUDD PILOSSOF

William Morrow and Company, Inc.

NEW YORK

It is the policy of William Morrow and Company, Inc., and its imprints and affiliates, recognizing the importance of preserving what has been written, to print the books we publish on acid-free paper, and we exert our best efforts to that end.

Library of Congress Cataloging-in-Publication Data
Schlesinger, Chris.
Salsas, sambals, chutneys & chowchows / by Chris Schlesinger and John Willoughby.
p. cm.
ISBN 0-688-12337-6
1. Condiments. 2. Cookery (Relishes) I. Willoughby, John.
II. Title. III. Title: Salsas, sambals, chutneys, and chowchows.
TX819.A1S34 1993
641.6'382—dc20 92-44696
CIP

Printed in the United States of America

First Edition

1 2 3 4 5 6 7 8 9 10

BOOK DESIGN BY BARBARA M. BACHMAN

To

Grandma Wetzler and

Grandma Schwyhart,

whose bountiful tables filled with pickles, relishes, jams, and "put-up" vegetables provided our first examples of the "little dishes" of the world. While this might seem like a book of exotic preparations, it all started back there.

CONTENTS

•

INTRODUCTION

EATING WITH RELISH—
SMALL PACKAGES,
BIG FLAVORS

•

This book came about because of a basic culinary rule of thumb: When you find something that is easy to make, healthful, and tastes great, go with it.

Well, the dishes in this book fill that bill precisely.

French cuisine may have its elaborate, subtle sauces, but the cuisines of the warm-weather world have their easygoing, carefree salsas . . . or chutneys, or sambals, or chowchows, or blatjangs, depending on the country in which you find them. The names attached to these "little dishes" are legion, but the concept stays the same: Healthful, easy-to-prepare, intensely flavored mixtures of fruits, vegetables, herbs, spices, and chile peppers bring culinary excitement to everyday eating around the world.

Fortunately, as the global village continues to shrink, we have all begun to appreciate the virtues of these concoctions. The bold, contrasting flavors of salsas, chutneys, and relishes are becoming more and more prevalent in our daily cooking. These dishes even seem to have dethroned pesto as the featured guest at restaurants and dinner parties alike. I am all in favor of this development, since I love these little dishes. But that doesn't mean I want to denigrate pesto. Far from it. In fact, it was this simple herb paste that first set me on the road to salsa madness.

It began one late-summer day in the final stages of my training as a professional chef at the Culinary Institute of America. My fellow students and I were in class preparing dinner from our repertoire, which consisted almost entirely of the classic French dishes of Escoffier, based on the elaborate mother sauce system. As usual, we had labored diligently all day with the myriad stocks, reductions, veloutés, and pan sauces of that cuisine.

But that day the chef, an Italian, called me over to his side. "Little Elephant," he said—he called me Little Elephant in deference to his opinion that I instantly forgot everything he tried to teach me, a flaw he seemed to enjoy, as there was always a hint of a smile on his face as he browbeat me mercilessly—"Little Elephant, go to the garden and get me a basketful of basil."

We had a huge herb garden at the Institute, and although I never saw anyone actually use its bounty, at least it looked nice. Heeding his admonition to pick only the tops, I walked over and gathered a mound of the pungent herb.

When I returned to the class, the chef personally oversaw the making of pasta pesto, a kind of treat for the students to enjoy before the weekend. It was no chore to make: Chop the basil, add garlic, pine nuts, olive oil, and salt and pepper, put in the pasta, go sneak some hard bread from the bakery, that's it. The real surprise came at the first bite—not only was this the easiest food I had made during my entire training, it was also the best. Its fresh, bright flavor far surpassed any of the complex sauces that our class had labored so diligently over during the semester, at least to my taste.

At the time, I thought it very ironic that a lot of money was being paid so I could learn the classic preparations, but the best thing I ate in my two years at the Institute was a pasta that took me about five minutes to make. It was as if the chef offered this dish up as a sort of Zen lesson for those who could understand—simple stuff tastes good.

Or maybe I just wanted to think that. Maybe the truth was that this dish was more in tune with my skills and sensibility, as I found rough-chopping a bunch of basil and a handful of garlic infinitely preferable to cutting carrots, celery, and onions into uniform sixteenth-inch cubes and adding them to a wonderfully subtle (read boring and bland) consommé which took about four hours to make and whose name I couldn't pronounce.

In any case, I took this particular lesson to heart. With traveling and work experience, my food knowledge and preferences grew, but the same scenario seemed to replay itself. I far preferred the salsas I found on my travels to Mexico, or the spicy, saladlike condiments my Asian co-workers brought to work with them, to the laborious concoctions that I was professionally trained and paid to create.

Hanging out on the beaches of Puerto Escondido, Mexico, for example, I found myself rapidly becoming addicted to the hot red tomato–chipotle salsa served in the beachfront restaurants. Similarly, on a trip to Bangkok, I ignored the city's fancy restaurants and spent hours wandering the streets, stopping at various stalls to sample one version after another of spicy, sweet-sour cucumber relish.

No doubt about it. The fancy sauces I prepared in fine dining rooms were simply no match in texture and flavor for the mixtures those guys on the beach or on the streets just chopped up and threw together.

As I began to collect examples of these "little dishes," I found that they share certain common characteristics. Whether you're talking about the ever-present green table salsa of Mexico, the combinations of fruit and fiery chile peppers of the West Indies, the sambals and chutneys of the Near and Far East, or the relishes, chowchows, and piccalillies of the American South, each individual mixture contains a whole batch of intense, loud, pungent, competing flavors. When you eat a spoonful, every taste bud in your mouth seems to light up in machine-gun succession. You taste sweet, then hot, then salt, then sour—then the whole shebang starts all over again, in a fraction of a second.

This wild intensity of flavor is the key to these dishes. With their dynamic, well-defined tastes, they can dress up a plain, well-cooked piece of meat or fish in a veritable Joseph's cloak of flavors, or turn simple beans, rice, or grains into a tasty, satisfying meal. Perhaps best of all, their vivid aromaticity, exotic ingredients, and spicy heat slake our growing thirst for culinary adventurism.

The virtues of these preparations are not limited just to great taste, however. In addition, they contain almost no cholesterol or fat, so they are more in line with the way we want to eat and cook today than are the rich sauces of classic European cuisines. But this doesn't mean they are "diet" foods, those lowered-fat substitutes that make you long for the real thing and feel deprived. Instead, these dishes are part of the "unconscious healthfulness" of many ethnic cuisines around the world. By this we mean that they were created not specifically to be healthful, but to be as tasty as possible using available ingredients. And because those ingredients are largely grain, legumes, fruits, vegetables, and spices, the resulting dishes turn out to be good for you.

But hold on—these dishes have yet another virtue: They are about the easiest things to prepare that you can imagine. Most require no more than chopping and mixing, or possibly a few minutes' use of a saucepan. Since they keep very well when covered and refrigerated, they also let you cook up a great meal in no time. Just toss a pork tenderloin on the grill or put a chicken in the oven, bring out the Avocado and Corn Salsa (page 15) or Sweet and Spicy Peach Relish (page 109) that you made over the weekend, and you're ready for an exciting, flavorful meal. A word of warning, though—if your dinner guests include any of your buddies who are into French cooking, don't tell them how easy this all is; it will just put them in a foul mood.

I also like the lack of any formal rules or prescriptions about which of these "little dishes" should be eaten with what. Since, unlike sauces, they have no organic connection to any particular entrée, they can be mixed and matched to suit individual tastes. The citrusy Banana-Lemon-Ginger Chutney (page 47) may go best with fish to your taste, while someone else may like it with chicken; you may think Sweet Carrot-Cucumber Sambal (page 69) is perfect when paired with grilled tuna, while a friend may prefer it on top of rice. In some of our recipes we have suggested ways you might use these dishes, but don't feel that you have to pay much attention to that. There's no right or wrong here, only the easy freedom of what tastes best to you.

There is a certain easy freedom, too, in the bewildering variety of names attached to these dishes. Unlike French recipes, which have been the subject of intense codification since the days of Carême and Escoffier, these dishes are part of folk culture, and their definitions are rather floating. If you spend a lot of time trying to define them precisely, you will only find the waters of confusion closing over your head. Translation is not a whole lot of help in sorting out which dish is what, for very often one label is simply transposed to another: The usual translation for the Spanish *salsa,* for example, is "sauce," and in Indian cookbooks the word "chutney" is most often translated into English as "relish."

Some of this linguistic confusion is a result of the intense culinary cross-fertilization that took place during the age of exploration and colonialism in the fifteenth and sixteenth centuries: Chile peppers from the Americas became deeply ingrained in the cuisines of many tropical countries; Malay-speaking indentured servants from the East Indies brought their chutneys and sambals with them to the Caribbean and southern Africa; African slaves brought their own foods and cooking techniques to the Americas; and so on.

This flow of new foods and preparations enriched cuisines everywhere, as indigenous cooks modified new recipes using their local ingredients. In southern Africa, for example, the shrimp pastes and mango pickles brought from Malaysia and Indonesia metamorphosed into the ubiquitous local blatjangs (vinegar-based mixtures) and atjars (similar mixtures based in fish oil).

The more research we did, the more we found that the individual names of these dishes result from the ingredients used in them, rather than from any type of technique or preparation. For example, a raw relish using typically Mexican ingredients is a salsa; with ingredients commonly found on the Pacific island of Java, it becomes a sambal; substitute classic Indian ingredients, and you've got a chutney.

In any case, a search for exactitude in nomenclature really misses the point of these easygoing dishes. Taking into account the multiplicity of regional and national preferences for this ingredient or that, we could simply say that one cook's sambal is another's chutney is another's relish.

Whatever you call them, the important attributes of these dishes remain the same—they are healthful, easy to prepare, and deliver intense flavors in small packages. This is food that lets you bring the vibrant tastes and strong, deep flavors of warm-weather cuisines into your own kitchens with very little effort. We like to think of them as vehicles to explore the unique tastes and flavor combinations of other cultures. So, go ahead—get in the driver's seat and let 'er rip.

SALSAS, SAMBALS, CHUTNEYS & CHOWCHOWS

SALSAS

Wild, Loose, and Loud

The most important thing to remember about salsas is that, like the Latin dance that shares their name, the best ones are wild, loose, and loud. But, just for fun, I'll try to come up with a definition, or at least a few guidelines, for what makes a salsa a salsa.

To most Americans, salsa conjures up the spicy, hot concoction based on tomatoes, onions, chile, and garlic that is known in Mexico as *Salsa Mexicana.* It is this tomato relish, in its many commercial guises, that recently sent tremors through the American gustatory world because its yearly sales outpaced that classic American condiment, tomato catsup.

I'm not sure if this is the harbinger of a great tidal wave of cultural realignment, as some experts seem to feel, but to most lovers of food it is a welcome change. Now that Americans have become accustomed to the vibrant flavors and spicy, chile-fueled edge of the table salsa of our southern amigos, we may be ready to move on to the many variations and permutations of this genre.

To me, salsas are simply the Mexican/Latin American version of the "little dishes" that this book is all about. What does this mean? Simply that salsas feature the vegetables, fruits, spices, and herbs characteristic of this region. Like their counterparts from other regions, they are often raw and full of intense, conflicting flavors. Since they come from the southern half of the Western Hemisphere, they usually include herbs like cilantro and oregano, spices like cumin and chili powder, and a range of vegetables and fruits from corn to tomatoes, jicama to pineapples, and mangoes to tomatillos. Lime juice and chile peppers are all but essential ingredients, with jalapeños leading the charge for the latter.

Of course, as with all the other definitions in this book, I don't worry about any of this too much. Just mix 'em up and enjoy the taste. In this case, everyone can dance.

I suggest you take the same loose and easy attitude toward the way you serve these salsas. You can serve them with any entrée from grilled fish to roast meats to stews. Use them to add lively, healthful flavor to steamed vegetables, or to brighten up heavier starch dishes like rice or beans. Of course, you can always just scoop them up with tortilla chips or deep-fried plantains or whatever is the scooping utensil of your choice. The point is, there are no rules here, so just suit yourself. You really can't go wrong.

BLACK BEAN AND PAPAYA SALSA WITH
TORTILLA CHIPS

Black Bean and Papaya Salsa

Makes about 5 cups

Black beans, a staple in the Latin world, have a dark, earthy flavor that we think goes very well with the rich flavor of papaya. And the color contrast makes a very colorful, festive look on the plate.

This Caribbean-inspired salsa is great with grilled fish, but it is also very tasty just by itself—as a spicy summer salad–type course, or scooped up with chips as a snack or appetizer.

Method: In a large mixing bowl, combine all the ingredients and mix together well.

This salsa will keep, covered and refrigerated, 4 to 5 days.

Note: For about 3 cups of cooked black beans: *Your Basic Black Beans:* Soak 2 cups dried black beans in cold water to cover overnight or for at least 5 hours, then drain and rinse well. In a large saucepan, heat 3 tablespoons peanut oil until hot but not smoking, then add 2 large yellow onions, diced, and sauté over high heat until clear, 4 to 5 minutes. Add 2 tablespoons minced garlic and sauté another minute, then add 1 teaspoon each of chili powder, ground cumin, Tabasco sauce, and sugar, along with ¼ cup white vinegar, 2 cups water, a bottle of your favorite beer, and the black beans. Bring to a simmer, cover well, and cook over low heat for 3 hours, or until the beans are soft to the bite. Don't overcook, or the beans will become mushy.

1 cup cooked or canned black beans (see Note)

2 ripe papayas, peeled, seeded, and diced small

½ red bell pepper, diced small

½ green bell pepper, diced small

½ red onion, diced small

¾ cup pineapple juice

½ cup lime juice (about 4 limes)

½ cup chopped cilantro

2 tablespoons ground cumin

1 tablespoon minced red or green chile pepper of your choice

Salt and freshly cracked black pepper to taste

SOFT TACOS WITH SHREDDED PORK AND
MANGO-TOMATILLO SALSA

MANGO-TOMATILLO SALSA

Makes about 6 cups

•

Here's another salsa that I discovered years ago on a visit to Mexico. The guy who was cooking at the Cabanas Tulum, a beachfront "hotel" in the Yucatán, had lived in California, and he demonstrated his creativity by adding mango to the classic Mexican green table salsa. I think the combination of the tart, lemon-herb flavor of the tomatillos and the rich smoothness of the mango is particularly tasty.

Bring this one out when you're making tacos. It also goes well with grilled Mexican pork dishes like *carnitas*.

Method: In a blender or food processor, purée the tomatillos, pineapple juice, vinegar, garlic, chiles, cilantro, cumin seeds, and lime juice. Place the mangoes, onions, and bell peppers in a medium bowl, add the purée, and mix well.

This salsa will keep, covered and refrigerated, 4 to 5 days.

1 12-ounce can tomatillos, drained

½ cup pineapple juice

¼ cup white vinegar

1 tablespoon minced garlic

1 tablespoon minced red or green chile pepper of your choice

½ cup chopped cilantro

2 tablespoons cumin seeds

6 tablespoons lime juice (about 3 limes)

3 ripe but firm mangoes, peeled, pitted, and diced small

1 red onion, diced small

1 red bell pepper, diced small

1 green bell pepper, diced small

TOASTING
CUMIN SEEDS

Toasting cumin seeds really brings out their flavor and aroma. To toast the seeds, heat a sauté pan over medium heat and place the seeds in it. Toast them, watching carefully and shaking frequently to avoid burning, until they just begin to release a little smoke, about 2 to 3 minutes. At this point you will also notice that the seeds begin to turn darker brown, and if you look carefully, some of them will be moving around a bit as the steam is released. That's all there is to it.

CUMIN SEEDS

RED TABLE SALSA WITH DEEP-FRIED
PLANTAIN ROUNDS

Puerto Escondido Salsa Roja de la Mesa

Makes about 4 cups

RED TABLE SALSA FROM THE LAND OF THE BIG WAVES

•

Early in my cooking career, I took off several months for a surfing trip through the Caribbean and the southern half of the Americas. Toward the end of this journey, I ended up in the beautiful village of Puerto Escondido on Mexico's Pacific coast. There I found myself instantaneously addicted to the hot red salsa, fueled by smoky chipotle peppers, that was routinely placed on the tables of the beachfront restaurants. This is my version of that classic condiment found in various guises throughout Mexico.

I advise you to put this out on the table at every meal, just as you do the salt and pepper. It's also an outstanding salsa for scooping up with tortilla chips or deep-fried plantain rounds.

3 large very ripe tomatoes, diced small

1 cup tomato juice

2 tablespoons minced chipotle peppers (see Pantry, page 133)

1 red onion, diced small

1 teaspoon minced fresh garlic

½ cup chopped fresh cilantro

½ cup lime juice (about 4 limes)

Salt and freshly cracked black pepper to taste

Method : Mix 'em together. That's it.

This salsa will keep, covered and refrigerated, about 5 to 6 days.

DEEP-FRIED PLANTAIN ROUNDS

Since we keep telling you that these are great for dipping with recipes in this book, we thought we'd also tell you how to make 'em. It's really easy: Peel 2 green plantains and cut them into 2-inch rounds. In a small saucepot, heat about 2 cups vegetable oil until hot but not smoking, then drop the plantain rounds into the oil, 3 or 4 at a time, and cook them until well browned, about 2 to 3 minutes. Remove them from the oil and drain on a paper bag. Next, stand each plantain round upright and smash it flat with a heavy object, like a frying pan. Put the smashed sections back into the oil, a few at a time, and cook about 2 minutes, or until the entire surface is golden brown. Remove them, drain, season with salt and pepper, and use as scoops for your favorite salsa.

DEEP-FRIED PLANTAIN ROUNDS

AVOCADO AND CORN SALSA WITH
GRILLED SHRIMP

Avocado and Corn Salsa

•

When someone says "salsa," we Americans usually think of the classic tomato-based red table salsa found throughout Mexico. That concoction is justly famed, but it is just the beginning of salsas, even in Mexico. For example, as Rick Bayless points out in his wonderful cookbook *Authentic Mexican* (Morrow), chunky guacamole is really an avocado salsa.

This version of salsa combines a number of typical Mexican ingredients—corn, avocado, chile peppers, oregano, cumin, lime—with the acidity of the lime juice just balancing the rich, loamy taste of the avocados.

It is great with grilled shrimp or other seafood. Or you might want to set it out, along with a couple of other salsas from this book and some chips and tortillas, as a kind of "salsa bar" appetizer.

Method: Blanch the corn in boiling water for 3 minutes, drain and cool under cold water. Cut the kernels off the cobs and mix together with all the remaining ingredients in a medium-sized bowl.

This salsa will keep, covered and refrigerated, about 2 to 3 days.

3 ears corn, husked and desilked (about 2 cups kernels)

3 ripe but firm avocados, peeled, pitted, and diced large

1 red onion, diced small

1 red bell pepper, diced small

⅓ cup virgin olive oil

¼ cup red wine vinegar

1 tablespoon minced garlic

4 to 8 shots Tabasco, depending on your dependency

1 tablespoon ground cumin

1 teaspoon chili powder

¼ cup chopped fresh oregano

½ cup lime juice (about 4 limes)

Salt and freshly cracked black pepper to taste

PAPAYA SALSA WITH GRILLED SEA SCALLOPS

PAPAYA SALSA

•

This is one of my favorites—healthful, quick, colorful, and full of intense flavors that cover the waterfront from sweet to sour to hot to smooth. Partially this is due to the character of the papaya, whose musky flavor mixes and mingles so well with other tropical ingredients. In any case, this is the kind of mixture that got me hooked on salsas to begin with.

This is a salsa recipe from central casting—you can substitute any fruit you have around, from peaches to mangoes to pineapples.

I think this is great with almost anything, but for starters, try it with seafood.

Method: In a large bowl, mix all the ingredients together well.

This salsa will keep, covered and refrigerated, 3 to 4 days.

1 ripe papaya, peeled, seeded, and roughly chopped

1 small red bell pepper, sliced into short, thin slices

1 small red onion, sliced into long, thin slices

¼ cup chopped fresh cilantro

1 medium clove garlic, minced

¼ cup pineapple juice

6 tablespoons lime juice (about 3 limes)

1 jalapeño pepper, finely chopped

Salt and freshly cracked black pepper to taste

ROASTED HABANERO SALSA FROM HELL
WITH GARGANELLI

ROASTED HABANERO SALSA FROM HELL

1 tablespoon plus ¼ cup virgin olive oil

1 teaspoon minced garlic

6 ripe plum tomatoes, halved

Salt and freshly cracked black pepper to taste

10 habanero chile peppers, stems removed

¼ cup lime juice (about 2 limes)

¼ cup chopped cilantro

Okay, heat lovers, this one's for you. If you think that jalapeño peppers make a nice snack when eaten by the handful, and your favorite culinary comment is "Nah, that's not really hot," then whip up a batch of this and take a big bite.

For the rest of us, a little of this baby goes a long way. The fuel here is the habanero, or Scotch Bonnet, the hottest chile pepper known to humankind. Fortunately, it is also the most flavorful, with a distinctive taste and a pungent, nasal heat. Instead of making the back of your throat burn, like many other chiles do, this one goes right to your head. To me, there's nothing better.

You might want to try mixing this with plain pasta, using about a tablespoon per serving—you'll still get a good dose of heat.

Method: In a small bowl, combine the tablespoon of olive oil and garlic and mix well. Rub the tomato halves with this mixture, sprinkle them with salt and freshly cracked pepper, and roast in a 500°F oven until they begin to take on some serious color, about 15 to 20 minutes. Remove them from the oven, allow to cool to room temperature, and dice.

Meanwhile, grill the habanero peppers over a medium-hot fire until slightly colored, 2 to 3 minutes. Remove the peppers from the fire and mince. (*Be very careful* when working with this pepper. Wear gloves when mincing it, and if you get any of the

(continued)

juice on your skin, wash it off with a mild bleach solution, which neutralizes the capsaicin. Also, be sure you don't rub your eyes while working with these peppers, and wash your hands well after you're done. These little guys are incendiary.)

In a medium-sized bowl, combine the tomatoes, peppers, ¼ cup of olive oil, lime juice, and cilantro, mix well, and prepare for takeoff.

This salsa will keep, covered and refrigerated, about 5 to 6 days, mainly because no mold or bacteria would dare to come near the stuff.

CHILE PEPPER ANTIDOTES

If your tolerance for heat is less than you thought it was—

or if you just underestimated the power of the habanero—

you might want to try one of the following antidotes to

cool off your mouth. Each has its own adherents, so you'll

just have to experiment to see which works best for you.

Chocolate • Milk • Corn bread or other

breads • Rice • Pasta • Sugar • Vintage

port • Orange Creamsicles (the personal favorite of

K. C. O'Hara, chef at the East Coast Grill)

SMOKED CORN AND CHILE SALSA WITH ROOT
VEGETABLE CHIPS

CORN AND CHILE SALSA AHUMADO

SMOKED CORN AND CHILE SALSA

•

Mexico is generally credited by historians as the original home of corn, or maize, as it is called throughout the rest of the world. Whatever the case may be, it is indisputable that corn goes very well with another major ingredient of Mexican cooking, the ubiquitous chile pepper.

In this salsa, we bring these two New World buddies together once again, combining smoky, lightly grilled corn with the rich, smoky flavor of chipotles, which are dried, smoked jalapeño peppers. If you are making this in the winter and don't like grilling in the snow, you can boil the corn for 1 to 2 minutes instead of grilling it, but you will lose some of the ineffable charred flavor.

Method: Rub the corn lightly with the vegetable oil and sprinkle lightly with salt and freshly cracked pepper. Grill over a low fire. To check the fire temperature, hold your hand about 5 inches above the grilling surface. If you can hold it there for 1 to 2 seconds, you have a hot fire; 3 to 4 seconds, a medium fire; and 5 to 6 seconds, a low fire. Longer than that, and your fire is too cool. Roll the ears around with your tongs to be sure they cook evenly, until the corn is slightly charred, about 7 to 10 minutes. Remove the ears from the grill and, as soon as they are

(continued)

Makes about 3 cups

4 ears corn, husked and desilked

1 tablespoon vegetable oil

Salt and freshly cracked black pepper to taste

4 scallions, ends removed and thinly sliced

1 red bell pepper, seeded and finely diced

2 tablespoons minced chipotle peppers (see Pantry, page 133)

2 tablespoons sugar

¼ cup cider vinegar

cool enough to handle, slice the kernels off the cobs. In a large bowl, mix the kernels with all the remaining ingredients.

This salsa will keep, covered and refrigerated, 3 to 4 days.

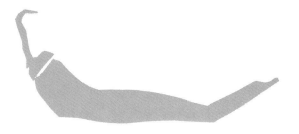

CHIPOTLES ARE YOUR FRIENDS

The chipotle, which is a dried, smoked jalapeño pepper, is a great cooking pepper. A kind of rough-and-ready chile, it has a deep, smoky flavor that goes with everything, and (very important for novice chile cooks) a consistent heat level. It is also relatively easy to find in its jarred or canned incarnation, which I find more satisfactory than the straight dried version. I recommend you get to know this chile well.

CLOCKWISE FROM LEFT: JALAPEÑO, CANNED
CHIPOTLE IN ADOBE SAUCE, AND
DRIED CHIPOTLE

CLAM SALSA WITH SALTINES AND TABASCO

ELMER'S EL SALVADOREAN CLAM SALSA

Makes about 2 cups

I call this a salsa because the guy who first made it for me loved to listen to salsa music. He was from El Salvador, and his job at the restaurant was to make sure all the food was received in good order. When the clams would come in, he'd always pick up a few and put them off to one side, then work on them over the next couple of hours, shucking the clams and chopping them as he got the chance, squeezing the lime, adding the Tabasco. When lunchtime rolled around, he'd eat this mixture with crackers like a kind of clam cocktail.

Every so often, if I had given him some help during the morning, I'd find a little bowl on my cutting board. It was always a treat, so I did my best to help him out whenever possible.

This is good as a dip with chips and also makes a daring but tasty combination with chicken—or, in the true style of Elmer himself, with saltines.

Method: In a medium-sized bowl, combine all the ingredients and mix well.

This salsa will keep, covered and refrigerated, about 2 days, but is best eaten right away.

1 cup minced fresh littleneck clams (about 18 to 20 medium-sized clams) or whatever variety is freshest in your locality

⅓ cup lime juice (about 2½ limes)

1 teaspoon minced garlic

½ red onion, diced small

5 radishes, diced small

1 ripe tomato, diced small

¼ cup chopped cilantro

6 to 10 shots Tabasco sauce, depending on your desire for heat

Salt and freshly cracked black pepper to taste

While shucking clams is not as easy as shelling peas, it isn't all that tough.

To shuck, get a clam and hold it flat side down in the palm of your hand, with the hinge resting against the ball of your thumb. Next, grab the clam knife with your other hand and line up the blade along the groove between the clam's shells opposite the hinge. Now, here's the big secret: Rather than trying to push the knife between the shells, curl the three middle fingers of the hand that is holding the clam over the dull side of the knife and *pull* the blade between the shells.

Once the blade is in, twist the wrist of the hand holding the knife so that the shell opens a bit, slide the knife along the inside of the top shell to sever the top muscle, then cut the back muscle at the hinge. Break off the top shell, sever the bottom muscle, and there you have it. Remove any grit.

What Do You Call That Again?

•

In the course of trying to distinguish one "small dish" from another, we traveled to a lot of places, read a lot of books, and talked to a lot of people. Here are some of the definitions that we found:

SALSA. Whether in books or in conversation, "salsa" is invariably translated into English as "sauce." You know what this one is, though.

SAMBAL. A paste of chiles and spices or a mixture of fruits or vegetables, raw or cooked, seasoned with spices and hot chiles—it depends on the country in which you ask the question.

CHUTNEY. Most experts just throw up their hands and cross-index chutney under "relish." Everyone agrees that a chutney enhances flavor and is somewhere in the neighborhood of a condiment, not quite a pickle, and not exactly a side dish.

CHOWCHOW and **PICCALILLI.** The first is sourer, the second is sweeter, but both are mixtures of vinegar, spices, and vegetables, usually including green tomatoes, used as a side dish or relish.

CATSUP. If you ask any American ten-year-old, you will be told that catsup is that tomatoy stuff you put on everything you eat. But if you check out old cookbooks and vintage restaurant menus, you'll find catsup to be any vinegar-based, spicy condiment with a vegetable or fruit as the main ingredient.

RELISH. All of the above.

Had enough? We have. Our advice is that you just make the stuff, call it whatever you want, and enjoy the great tastes.

CHUTNEYS

THE ORIGINAL RELISH?

•

Say "chutney," and many Americans will reply—or at least think of—"Major Grey." This is because the good major's mango pickle chutney is a marketer's dream: A brand name that has become virtually synonymous in the public mind with the generic product of which it is a single example. However, just as we have learned to say "tissue" instead of "Kleenex," and "copier" rather than "Xerox," so Americans are starting to explore the nearly infinite variety of chutneys, the little dishes of India and the region surrounding the subcontinent.

Chutneys have a fair claim to be the first of the "little dishes" that this book is all about. However, the spread of this concept throughout much of the world is a complicated phenomenon, and there are probably almost equally persuasive champions of the sambal, the salsa, and many other variants. In fact, with a culinary idea this useful and this universal, little dishes of the chutney variety just may have occurred simultaneously to cooks all around the world, so each claim of originality may be as valid as the next.

Even in their home country of India, chutneys are a varied lot. They may be either raw or cooked, and range from chunky combinations of fruits, vegetables, and spices to rather plain affairs of grated vegetables with a few other flavors. As Julie Sahni points out in her excellent cookbook *Classic Indian Vegetarian and Grain Cooking* (Morrow), chutneys that contain large chunks of fruits or vegetables, like Major Grey's and most of those included here, might be considered pickles in India.

In this chapter, we have included both cooked and raw chutneys, relying on a variety of fruits, vegetables, spices, and herbs. Two things will become apparent as you go through them—First, I really like ginger in chutneys. And second, as you might have guessed, what all these chutneys have in common is that they are easy to make, healthful, and taste great.

These chutneys go well with spicy foods, since they follow the mold of the original versions, designed to go with curries. We think they are also great with roasted meats and game, and would not hesitate to pair them with just about anything grilled.

GREEN MANGO–CARROT CHUTNEY WITH GINGER
AND CORIANDER

Green Mango–Carrot Chutney with Ginger and Coriander

Makes about 3 ½ cups

While we usually think of chutneys as being cooked, they can also be raw. In tropical climates, mangoes and similar fruits are used as vegetables when green and as fruits when ripe. Here, the firmness and slight tartness of the green mangoes give this chutney a distinctive texture and taste.

This one can go with anything, but it's just as good by itself as a side dish/salad kind of thang.

Method: Using the largest holes of your kitchen grater, shred the mangoes and carrots. Mix together with the remaining ingredients in a large bowl. Allow to stand, covered, for about 1 hour before serving so the tastes mingle and mellow.

This chutney will keep, covered and refrigerated, about 4 days.

3 green mangoes, peeled and sliced off the pit

1 large carrot, peeled and the ends trimmed off

1 tablespoon minced fresh ginger

1 teaspoon minced garlic

½ cup red wine vinegar

3 tablespoons molasses

1 tablespoon coriander seeds, crushed

2 tablespoons lime juice (about 1 lime)

Salt and freshly cracked black pepper to taste

It's a Fruit,
It's a Vegetable,
It's Two Ingredients
in One

Firmer in texture and less sweet than ripe specimens, green mangoes are ideal for use as an unusual and flavorful vegetable. This is fortunate because, since the fruit does not ship well, it is easier to find good-quality green mangoes than ripe ones in supermarkets in the United States. They are more readily available here in the summertime, because that is the mango season in Florida. However, imports are available most of the year, since they are pretty much a year-round crop in the countries from which they are shipped here.

GREEN MANGOES

FRIED ONION-GINGER CHUTNEY WITH GRILLED
SHELL STEAK

FRIED ONION–GINGER CHUTNEY

Frying the onions adds an underlying sweetness to this chutney, which features the combination of hot, sweet, and sour tastes so typical of equatorial cuisines. Be bold but cautious when frying—the onions take on a distinctive, sweet, rich taste when they become dark brown, but you want to be sure not to let them burn and turn black.

For this chutney, give me a big old rare steak and a jug of red wine.

Method : In a large frying pan, heat the olive oil over medium-high heat until hot but not smoking. Fry the onions 7 to 9 minutes, stirring constantly, until dark brown. Add the garlic and ginger and cook 1 additional minute. Add all the remaining ingredients and cook an additional 5 minutes, stirring occasionally. Remove from the heat, cool, and serve.

This chutney will keep, covered and refrigerated, about 1 week.

2 tablespoons virgin olive oil

2 white onions, peeled and very thinly sliced

1 tablespoon minced garlic

2 tablespoons minced fresh ginger

2 whole star anise, crushed

1 tablespoon curry powder

1/8 teaspoon ground mace (you may substitute ground cinnamon)

2 tablespoons each molasses, orange juice, and white vinegar

Salt and freshly cracked white pepper to taste

We love star anise, not only for its spicy aroma and licorice flavor, but also because it just looks great. This eight-pointed, star-shaped spice is actually the seedpod of an Asian evergreen tree. As the pod is dried, each of the "arms" of the star splits open to reveal a tiny brown seed in its point. Decorative, aromatic, delicious—you can't ask much more of a spice.

STAR ANISE

K.C.'S DRIED FRUIT CHUTNEY WITH ROAST RACK OF LAMB

K.C.'s Dried Fruit Chutney

The sweet, rather intense flavors of dried fruits are a natural for chutneys. K. C. O'Hara, the tall and talented chef at the East Coast Grill, developed this particular version in which you dry your own fruits in the oven. This is much easier than you might think, and it gives you a more tender chutney. Besides, leaving fruit in a low oven overnight creates a delicate, sweet aroma that is almost as nice to wake up to as the smell of coffee. Almost.

This is a very versatile chutney, good with sandwiches and all types of roasted meats. My favorite way to use it is with any type of lamb.

Method : Split the fruits in half, rub them very lightly with vegetable oil, and sprinkle with salt and pepper. Place them in a single layer on a cooling rack set on top of a sheet pan, and slow-bake in a 200°F oven overnight, or for about 8 hours. The finished products should be about half the size of the originals, wrinkled and slightly firm to the touch, but with no dramatic change of color.

In a heavy sauté pan or saucepan, sauté the onions in 2 tablespoons of vegetable oil until transparent, about 5 to 7 minutes. Add the dried fruits and stir and cook for 2 to 3 more minutes.

Add all the remaining ingredients except the vinegar, lemon juice, and mint, bring to a simmer, and simmer over low heat for about 1 hour, stirring occasionally. You may need to add a small amount of water or orange juice if the mixture begins to stick to the bottom of the pan.

(continued)

8 ripe peaches, plums, or nectarines

Vegetable oil for oiling fruit, about 3 tablespoons

Salt and freshly cracked black pepper to taste

Vegetable oil for sautéing onions, about 2 tablespoons

2 large onions, diced small

1 medium red bell pepper, diced small

6 tablespoons brown sugar

1/4 cup white sugar

1 tablespoon molasses

1/4 cup raisins

1/2 cup orange juice

1 teaspoon salt

1/2 teaspoon freshly cracked black pepper

1/2 teaspoon coriander seeds, lightly toasted, then cracked

1/2 cup white vinegar

2 tablespoons lemon juice (about 1/2 lemon)

1 teaspoon freshly chopped mint

Remove from the heat, allow to cool, and add the vinegar, lemon juice, and mint. Mix well and serve.

This chutney will keep, covered and refrigerated, about 3 weeks.

CHUTNEY SHORTCUT

To save some time, you can also make a perfectly delicious version of this chutney using store-bought dried fruits. Peaches, pears, apples, or some combination thereof are easy to find and make an excellent chutney.

To use store-bought fruits, follow the recipe just as written, starting with the sautéing of the onions, but add ½ cup of water to the mixture at the point at which you add the vinegar, lemon juice, and mint. Other than that, it's the same drill.

TOASTING CORIANDER SEEDS

Toasting coriander seeds not only brings out their flavor and aroma, it also gives your kitchen an exotic, enticing smell. We highly recommend it.

To toast the seeds, heat a sauté pan over medium heat and place the seeds in it. Toast them, watching carefully and shaking frequently to avoid burning, until they become aromatic, darken slightly, and just begin to release a little smoke, about 2 to 3 minutes.

CORIANDER SEEDS

BANANA-LEMON-GINGER CHUTNEY WITH
GRILLED QUAIL

BANANA-LEMON-GINGER CHUTNEY

Malay-speaking people brought to Africa as slaves brought their relishes and chutneys with them. Later, Indian immigrants to South and East Africa added their versions to the repertoire. As always, local ingredients and cooking traditions brought changes to the original recipes, and a whole range of new chutneys were created.

This chutney, in the East African tradition, features the bananas and aromatic spices central to the cooking of that region. It is best to use bananas that are just slightly underripe, since they keep their shape better. But don't use really green ones, or you will end up with a bitter, chalky chutney.

This is particularly good with roasted or grilled game, such as rabbit, duck, or quail.

Method: In a large sauté pan, heat the peanut oil over high heat until hot but not smoking. Add the onion slices and sauté, stirring occasionally, until translucent, about 5 to 6 minutes. Lower the heat to medium, add the ginger, and sauté an additional 1 minute. Add all the remaining ingredients, bring to a simmer, reduce heat to low, and cook until the liquid is about as thick as catsup, about 10 to 15 minutes.

This chutney will keep, covered and refrigerated, about 2 weeks.

1 tablespoon peanut oil

1 onion, thinly sliced

1 tablespoon minced fresh ginger

4 almost-ripe bananas, cut into 1-inch-thick rounds

½ cup brown sugar

¼ cup fresh lemon juice (about 1 lemon)

¼ cup red wine vinegar

¼ cup orange juice

Pinch each of ground mace, ground nutmeg, ground cloves, and ground cinnamon

Salt and freshly cracked black pepper to taste

CURRIED PINEAPPLE AND GINGER CHUTNEY
OVER COUSCOUS

CURRIED PINEAPPLE AND GINGER CHUTNEY

•

Pineapple and ginger are one of those combinations that just seem to work well together; add curry powder, and you've got a time-proven flavorful taste provider.

I like to eat this chutney for lunch with plain boiled rice or even couscous. I think the combination makes a clear case for the satisfying, flavorful nature of a diet largely based on grains but combined with some type of intensely flavored side dish for wild tastes.

Method: In a 4-quart saucepan, heat the oil over medium-high heat until hot but not smoking. Add the bell peppers and onions and sauté, stirring constantly, until the onions start to become translucent, about 5 to 6 minutes.

Add the ginger, garlic, chile peppers, and curry powder and sauté 1 minute more. Add all the remaining ingredients except the salt and pepper and bring to a boil. Reduce the heat to low and simmer for 10 to 15 minutes, stirring occasionally, until the liquid has thickened slightly. Season with salt and freshly cracked black pepper to taste, remove from the heat, and allow to cool to room temperature.

This chutney will keep, covered and refrigerated, about 2 weeks.

¼ cup vegetable or peanut oil for sautéing

1 red bell pepper, cut into ½-inch squares

1 green bell pepper, cut into ½-inch squares

1 red onion, peeled, halved, and cut into ½-inch squares

¼ cup minced fresh ginger

1 tablespoon minced garlic

1 tablespoon minced red or green chile pepper of your choice

3 tablespoons good quality curry powder

1 large pineapple, peeled, cored, and cut into ½-inch-square chunks (about 4 cups)

½ cup raisins

1½ cups white vinegar

½ cup orange or pineapple juice

1 cup brown sugar

Salt and freshly cracked black pepper to taste

BLATJANGS, ATJARS, AND SAMBALS

WHEN WORLDS COLLIDE

•

These recipes are grouped together because they all have names not in your average American's vocabulary—and because they share some common history. To me, they provide a fascinating illustration of the ways that dishes migrate among cultures. They also serve to show that there is little point in struggling to strictly classify these dishes by name.

Blatjangs are chutneylike accompaniments widely used in the Malay cuisine of South Africa. Oddly enough, these mixtures trace their ancestry to a paste of fermented shrimp or prawns, which was brought to Africa in the seventeenth century by Malay-speaking people from the East Indies. (Some historians say the Malays were brought to serve the Dutch colonists as indentured servants, others call them slaves; whichever the case, they were definitely not coming to South Africa on a pleasure cruise.) In fact, in Malaysia even today shrimp paste is known as *belacan,* which sounds exactly like "blatjang" when pronounced by a Malay speaker.

In southern Africa, however, the term gradually came to stand for accompaniments containing prawn paste, rather than the paste itself, and eventually metamorphosed to encompass the chutneyesque blatjangs of today, most of which contain no shrimps or prawns at all. Instead, they are spicy mixtures of chiles, other spices, and the fruits and vegetables of southern Africa, such as apricots, dates, and eggplants.

Atjars, too, came from the East Indies to Africa. The term originally denoted a type of mango pickle commonly made on the Indonesian island of Java. Over the years, South African cooks widened the expression to include many types of vegetables preserved in oil that had been boiled with spices. Meanwhile, cooks in Indonesia had also been expanding their concept of atjar—or *acar,* as they more commonly spell it—over the centuries. As in southern Africa, the term "acar" in Malaysia and Indonesia now applies to a wide range of preserved vegetable and spice mixtures.

The Malays brought yet another mixture to Africa with them, this one known as the sambal. In the Malay-derived cooking of today's southern Africa, sambals are commonly understood to be condiments of raw, grated fruits or vegetables seasoned with vinegar and chiles.

In the Southeast Asian nations where they originated, sambals are also major culinary players. There, however, the term has a much wider range of meaning. In Malaysia, for example, one of the most common sambals is simply shrimp paste and fried chile peppers pounded together with a mortar and pestle. Many other sambals are cooked, usually by frying; these versions contain a wide variety of ingredients, from coconut to squid to eggplant. Finally, sambals can also be uncooked mixtures of these same ingredients, in which case the emphasis is on fruits and vegetables, along with the requisite spices and chile peppers.

Does this all have a familiar ring? Once again, one cook's chutney is another's atjar is another's sambal.

As with all the dishes in this book, the ones in this chapter can be used in all sorts of ways. Atjars, for example, are basically pickles, so they make particularly good side munchies. Some of the preparations in this section, like the Malay Quince and Chile Sambal (page 67), may look like sweets, but don't make the mistake of trying to use them as a topping for pound cake or ice cream. Using fruits in savory preparations has a long tradition in many cultures, and as you try them I think you'll find it's a great way to use fruits of all kinds.

APRICOT-FIG BLATJANG WITH ITS RAW
INGREDIENTS

APRICOT-FIG BLATJANG

Makes about 3 cups

Blatjangs, those chutneylike dishes of southern Africa, are often based on dried fruits. Apricots and raisins, for example, are very popular ingredients. Here we have added figs, which are widely used in the cuisines of northern Africa, but you may substitute any dried fruits that you choose.

Like other blatjangs, this goes very well with any type of roasted meats or game. Personally, I favor this one with lamb.

Method: In a saucepan, combine the apricots, figs, raisins, onion, and vinegar with enough water to just cover. Bring to a boil, reduce the heat, and simmer for 15 to 20 minutes, stirring frequently, until the mixture is about the thickness of honey. (Do not overcook, as the mixture will thicken as it cools.) Remove from the heat.

Meanwhile, toast the almonds on a baking sheet in a 325°F oven for 8 to 10 minutes, or until just lightly browned.

In a food processor or blender, combine the ginger, chile peppers, almonds, and salt and pepper to taste, and purée well. Add the puréed spice mixture and the lemon juice to the apricot mixture and stir well.

This blatjang will keep, covered and refrigerated, up to 3 weeks.

3/4 pound (about 1½ cups) dried apricots

1/4 pound (about ½ cup) dried figs

1/4 pound (about ½ cup) golden raisins

1 small onion, diced small

1/2 cup cider vinegar

1/4 cup blanched almonds

1 tablespoon minced fresh ginger

1 teaspoon minced red or green chile pepper of your choice

Salt and freshly cracked white pepper to taste

1/4 cup lemon juice (about 1 lemon)

CHUNKY OVEN-DRIED TOMATO AND EGGPLANT
BLATJANG WITH GRILLED MEDALLIONS OF PORK
TENDERLOIN

CHUNKY OVEN-DRIED TOMATO AND EGGPLANT BLATJANG

Makes about 4 cups

Blatjangs, which are the South African version of chutneys, are usually ground into an almost smooth paste. However, I like the added texture that is provided when you use minced or chopped ingredients but don't mash them.

This is a fairly hot mixture, as blatjangs are supposed to be, but if you don't like your food too fiery you can just cut down on the amount of chile pepper.

I like eggplant with pork, so I might try this with a pork tenderloin. It goes well with chicken, too.

Method: Rub the tomato halves with the olive oil and sprinkle them generously with salt and pepper. Arrange them in a single layer on top of a rack placed on a large sheet pan, and slow-bake in a 190°F oven overnight, or about 8 hours. The tomatoes will shrink and shrivel up a bit, and their flavor will intensify. Remove them from the oven, chop roughly, and set aside.

Meanwhile, toss the diced eggplant and the ¼ cup of salt together in a large bowl until well mixed. Place the eggplant on a sheet pan and let stand at room temperature for 1 hour. Squeeze out the moisture by gently wringing it out in a kitchen towel or by pressing the eggplant lightly in a strainer.

In a large sauté pan, add 3 tablespoons of peanut oil (to cover the bottom of the pan) and heat over high heat until hot but not smoking. Add enough eggplant to cover the bottom of the pan in a single layer and sear until golden brown, about 2 minutes. Remove with a slotted spoon and set aside. Repeat with the

(continued)

12 ripe plum tomatoes, halved

¼ cup virgin olive oil

Salt and freshly cracked black pepper to taste

2 medium-sized unpeeled eggplants, diced into ½-inch squares

¼ cup salt

6 tablespoons peanut oil

1 onion, diced small

1 tablespoon minced fresh ginger

1 tablespoon minced garlic

2 tablespoons minced red or green chile pepper of your choice

½ cup golden raisins

1¼ cups red wine vinegar

⅓ cup brown sugar

1 tablespoon toasted, crushed coriander seeds

Salt and freshly cracked black pepper to taste

remaining eggplant. Add the remaining peanut oil, heat until hot but not smoking, and sauté the onions, stirring frequently, until they just begin to color, about 5 minutes. Reduce the heat to medium, add the ginger and garlic, and cook about 1 minute, stirring frequently. Add the reserved eggplant and tomatoes, along with all the remaining ingredients and bring the mixture to a simmer. Reduce the heat to low and cook an additional 5 minutes, stirring constantly. Remove from the heat and serve.

This blatjang will keep, covered and refrigerated, about 1 week.

OVEN-DRIED TOMATOES

Whether you're talking tomatoes or peaches or apples, drying fruit in your oven is not only easy, it also concentrates the fruit's flavor wonderfully and makes it easier to keep. So the next time you've got some fruit that is just a little on the edge, throw it in the oven.

To dry plum tomatoes, split them in half lengthwise, place them on a large drying rack set on top of a sheet pan, and sprinkle with salt and pepper and a bit of finely chopped rosemary or thyme. Place in a 190° F oven for about 8 hours, depending on the size and ripeness of the tomatoes. The tomatoes should be shriveled up and reduced to about half their original size when done. Their taste will be fantastic, rich and sweet and slightly acidic.

OVEN-DRIED PLUM TOMATOES

MIXED VEGETABLE ATJAR

MIXED VEGETABLE ATJAR

When Dutch colonists brought Malays from the East Indies to South Africa, a unique cross-cultural cuisine was born. South Africans picked up on the Javanese spicy condiment atjar and gave it many various incarnations, using the indigenous vegetables and spices available to them there.

In this atjar, we combine several vegetables in a colorful, flavorful mix. It makes an unusual side dish, and is also a great accompaniment to lamb or pork of any description. Try putting it out as a cocktail snack on a hot summer day.

Method : Fill your largest stockpot with water and bring it to a boil. Fill another large stockpot or bucket with ice water.

Blanch the carrots, cauliflower, and green beans separately for 1 minute each, removing them to the ice water as they are finished. When they are cool, rub them well with the salt, allow to stand for 1 hour, then rinse *very* well, drain, and pat dry.

Meanwhile, put the peanut oil in a very deep saucepan and heat over high heat until it just begins to simmer. Be careful that you do not allow it to go beyond this point, because if you let it boil unattended, you have the potential for an unmitigated disaster, especially if you are cooking with gas. As soon as the oil starts to simmer, turn off the heat, allow oil to cool 10 to 15 minutes, then add the mustard seeds, cumin, curry powder, coriander seeds, and cloves, and allow to cool for an additional 10 minutes.

Combine the drained vegetables, ginger, and onions, mix well, and pack the mixture into a jar or jars. Pour the hot spiced oil into the jars to fill completely. Bring mixture to room temperature prior to serving.

This atjar will keep, covered and refrigerated, almost indefinitely.

- 2 carrots, peeled and cut into ¼-inch rounds
- 1 cup cauliflower florets
- 20 green beans
- ¼ cup salt
- 2 cups peanut oil
- 1 tablespoon black mustard seeds (you may substitute yellow seeds)
- 1 tablespoon ground cumin
- 1 tablespoon curry powder
- 1 tablespoon coriander seeds, crushed
- 3 whole cloves
- 1 finger-sized section of ginger, peeled and sliced into dime-sized rounds
- 1 red onion, peeled, quartered, and separated into sections

CARROT-CUCUMBER ACAR WITH FRIED GARLIC
AND GRILLED PORK SKEWERS

CARROT-CUCUMBER ACAR WITH FRIED GARLIC

Makes about 4 cups

This is a variation on the Indonesian rendition of acars. In the vast complex of islands that make up this country, these mixtures of vegetables, vinegar, and spices are variously used as pickles, condiments, and salads. Frying garlic until it's light brown is a common technique in Indonesia, and I think it adds a very distinctive flavor to this acar. Be careful, though, not to let the garlic get dark brown or black, or it will turn bitter.

This acar goes very well with grilled chicken or with pork skewers; you might also try it as an accompaniment to a stew.

Method: Place the olive oil and garlic in a large frying pan and cook over medium heat, stirring frequently, until the garlic just turns light brown, 6 to 7 minutes. Add the ginger and spices and cook an additional 2 minutes, stirring constantly to prevent burning. Add the vinegar and sugar and cook another 3 minutes, stirring occasionally. Add the carrots, cucumber, and bell pepper slices, remove from the heat, and stir well. Season with salt to taste, then add the cilantro. Allow to come to room temperature, then refrigerate.

This acar will keep, covered and refrigerated, 4 to 5 days.

1/4 cup virgin olive oil

10 cloves garlic, thinly sliced

1 tablespoon minced fresh ginger

1 teaspoon each ground coriander, ground cumin, ground white pepper, ground nutmeg, and curry powder

1 cup white vinegar

1/2 cup brown sugar

1 cup small-diced carrots

2 smallish unpeeled cucumbers, cut in half lengthwise, then in thin disks

1 red bell pepper, very thinly sliced

Salt to taste

1/4 cup chopped fresh cilantro

SAMBAL IN THE STYLE OF JAVA WITH GRILLED CHICKEN SKEWERS

SAMBAL IN THE STYLE OF JAVA

Java is one of the largest and most populous of the more than 13,600 islands that make up the nation of Indonesia. In the western part of this island, salads of raw vegetables are very popular, and like most other Javanese dishes they often feature chile peppers, peanuts, and sweet-sour taste combinations. Now, you might think that this dish has a weird combination of tastes, but go ahead and tell your friends what's in it before they take their first bite, then just sit back and wait for the usual reaction—"Wow, that's a great combination."

You can vary the taste of this dish by changing the type of bean sprouts you use; soy sprouts give a thicker texture, radish sprouts add a peppery taste, etc. This works really well as a side dish for satés of all kinds.

Method: In a very large bowl, combine the cabbage, carrots, bean sprouts, and peanuts. In a separate bowl, combine all the dressing ingredients and, in a food processor or blender, process until very well blended. Pour the dressing over the vegetables and mix well.

This sambal will keep, covered and refrigerated, 2 days, but is best eaten shortly after it is made.

2 cups shredded green cabbage

1 cup peeled, shredded carrots (about 1 large or 2 small carrots)

½ cup bean sprouts of your choice

½ cup peanuts, toasted

THE DRESSING

1 tablespoon minced fresh ginger

1 tablespoon minced red or green chile pepper of your choice

1 teaspoon minced garlic

1 teaspoon shrimp paste (see Pantry, page 146)

2 tablespoons coriander seeds, cracked

¼ cup lime juice (about 2 limes)

¼ cup sugar

¼ cup soy sauce

¼ cup molasses

½ cup peanut oil

Salt and freshly cracked black pepper to taste

MALAY QUINCE-CHILE SAMBAL OVER HACKED
ROAST DUCK

MALAY QUINCE-CHILE SAMBAL

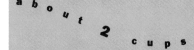

This is my version of a classic sambal from the Malay cuisine of South Africa. Quinces, with their distinctive dryish texture and rather sour taste, are a staple in this area of Africa, and quince sambals are considered the ideal accompaniment for roast meats. If quinces of good quality are not available in your area, though, you can substitute unpeeled Granny Smith apples.

Try this one with roast duck or goose; the fatty birds benefit from the acidity of the sambal. In other words, if your goose is cooked, use this on it.

Method: Grate the quinces or apples and mix them together with the salt in a medium-sized bowl. Allow to stand for about ½ hour, then squeeze out any excess liquid that has accumulated. Combine the grated fruit with all the remaining ingredients and mix well.

This sambal will keep, covered and refrigerated, about 1 week.

- 4 quinces, peeled and cored (you may substitute 4 Granny Smith apples)
- 1 tablespoon salt
- ¼ cup white vinegar
- ¼ cup lemon juice (about 1 lemon)
- 1 tablespoon minced red or green chile pepper of your choice
- 1 teaspoon minced garlic
- 1 teaspoon sugar
- 1 teaspoon minced fresh ginger

SWEET CARROT-CUCUMBER SAMBAL WITH CHILES
AND FISH SAUCE OVER STEAMED RICE

Sweet Carrot-Cucumber Sambal with Chiles and Fish Sauce

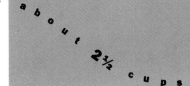

Makes about 2½ cups

Throughout Southeast Asia, cooks have created a whole range of side dishes and condiments known collectively as sambals. This version combines the cucumber, carrots, fresh aromatic herbs, and fermented fish sauce that are primary ingredients of Southeast Asian cooking, along with the essential chile peppers.

You might want to try this with a flavorful grilled fish, maybe a tuna steak or bluefish fillet. Or, for a quick, healthful, tasty meal, try it with plain rice, the way it is most commonly eaten in its place of origin.

Method: In a medium-sized bowl, combine all the ingredients and mix well.

This sambal will keep, covered and refrigerated, 1 to 2 days.

1 unpeeled cucumber, cut in half lengthwise and thinly sliced

½ large carrot, peeled and grated

½ red onion, diced small

1 tablespoon of your favorite minced red or green chile pepper (you may substitute 2 teaspoons of red pepper flakes)

½ cup white vinegar

2 tablespoons sugar

1 tablespoon each chopped cilantro, chopped fresh mint, and chopped fresh basil

1 tablespoon fermented fish sauce (available in Southeast Asian stores)

Salt and freshly cracked black pepper to taste

Fish sauce is as ubiquitous in the cuisines of Southeast Asia as salt is in American food. Made from the drippings of salted, fermented fish, this condiment is called *nuoc mam* in Vietnam, *nam pla* in Thailand, *nam pa* in Laos, and so on. It is something of an acquired taste, but once you get over what may be an initial squeamish reaction, it quickly becomes almost addictive. When you leave it out of a dish that calls for it, you will miss the depth and undercurrents of flavor that it adds.

For those of you who might think that such a product is too gross for words, we refer you to the ancient Greeks and Romans, so often held up as the ideal models of good taste. They used a similar condiment, which they called *garum.* The only difference was, they fermented small fish together with the intestines of larger fish to make this sauce, which they used in all kinds of dishes.

FISH SAUCE

CUCUMBER-PINEAPPLE SAMBAL WITH KEBABS OF
BEEF TENDERLOIN AND RED BELL PEPPER

CUCUMBER-PINEAPPLE SAMBAL

•

This dish showcases the combination of vegetable, fruit, sweet, and hot tastes representative of the sambals of Indonesia. Clean, crisp raw cucumber is often used to balance sweet or hot tastes. We're making this one a little more intense with the heavy sweetness of molasses and the punch of chiles. The heat has been toned down for Western tastes, but feel free to increase the amount of chile pepper if you like it.

Serve this with grilled skewered meat, fish, or vegetables of any kind. To further play on the peanut theme, serve up some Sambal in the Style of Java (page 65) along with it.

Method: In a medium-sized bowl, combine all the ingredients and mix well.

This sambal will keep, covered and refrigerated, 3 to 4 days.

- 2 cucumbers, peeled, seeded, and cut into small cubes

- 1 medium-sized pineapple, skinned, cored, and cut into small cubes

- ½ cup rice wine vinegar (you may substitute white vinegar)

- 2 tablespoons soy sauce

- 2 tablespoons molasses

- 2 tablespoons minced fresh ginger

- 1 or 2 minced red chile peppers of your choice, depending on your taste for heat (you may substitute ½ to 1 teaspoon red pepper flakes)

- Salt and freshly cracked white pepper to taste

CHOWCHOWS, PICCALILLIES, AND OTHER PICKLED THINGS

FLAVOR SAVERS

•

Pickles—fruits and vegetables preserved in vinegar, oil, or brine—have a long and illustrious history around the world. In fact, their exact origin is a bone of some contention, like many other aspects of folk culture that can't be strictly proven. For what it's worth, if I were to make a wager, I'd put ten bucks down on India as the first pickle producer.

In America, when you say pickles, many people's minds immediately run to the South or the Midwest of our own country. Surely these regions have a grand pickling past, but there are equally great pickling traditions in other countries from Korea, with its fermented kimchi, to Iran, with its pickled turnips, to South America, with its oil-preserved aji chile peppers. And let's not forget the barrooms of nineteenth-century America, where pickled eggs were among the favored "freebies."

In any case, what started out as a means of preserving perishable produce has created a whole magilla of great-tasting preparations. With modern refrigeration, it is no longer necessary to worry so much about preservation in and of itself, but the time-honored tart-sweet taste created by pickling can't be beat. Also, the fact that pickling, or "putting up," as it used to be called, is so strongly identified with industriousness and good, old-fashioned, hearty homemade food gives it a special appeal these days.

In this section, we have included variations on those two great pickled relishes of the American South, chowchows and piccalillies, along with a light version of kimchi, Korea's pickled, fermented cabbage, and spicy pickled grapes. None of these versions are meant to be sealed and kept indefinitely. Instead, they are designed to be kept for a few days to a few months, and aim to capture the flavor and style of pickles and pickled relishes, rather than their longevity. After all, few of us are likely to need pickled fruits and vegetables as vitamin sources on months-long ocean voyages or Crusades to the Holy Lands, but we still love the way they taste.

GREEN CABBAGE-CORN CHOWCHOW

GREEN CABBAGE–CORN CHOWCHOW

Makes about 4 cups

1 cup diced green cabbage

Kernels from 3 ears corn, uncooked

1 red bell pepper, diced small

1 green bell pepper, diced small

1 red onion, diced small

½ cup diced celery

5 whole cloves

2 cups cider vinegar

¼ cup sugar

Salt and freshly cracked black pepper to taste

The term "chowchow" has a vaguely Chinese sound—or, more correctly, it sounds like the pidgin English that extras in Charlie Chan movies used to speak. In fact, some experts say that the word derives from the pidgin English term for "mixture" and was brought to the United States by Chinese laborers in the nineteenth century. However, we have found it in a recipe book of a seventeenth-century Virginia housewife, so who knows?

In any case, today chowchow has come to mean a sourish combination of vegetables preserved in vinegar and usually containing cabbage. It's one of those things that every Southern and Midwestern grandma worth her salt used to "put up."

This is a great picnic side dish. Or, if you are the sort who likes to bring something with you when you go to a friend's house for dinner, a jar of this will certainly fit the bill.

Method: Prepare all the vegetables as described and place them in a large mixing bowl. Combine the cloves, vinegar, sugar, and salt and freshly cracked pepper to taste in a saucepan and bring to a boil over high heat. Pour this mixture over the vegetables, mix very well, let stand until it has reached room temperature, then cover and refrigerate.

This chowchow will keep, covered and refrigerated, about 3 weeks.

SWEET GREEN TOMATO AND CORN PICCALILLI

SWEET GREEN TOMATO AND CORN PICCALILLI

Makes about 6 cups

•

Piccalilli is the name Southerners give to most any type of relish that includes green tomatoes along with other vegetables. Often "piccalilli" is used interchangeably with "chowchow," another Southern relish tradition. To my perspective, though, it seems that piccalilli is usually rather sweet, while cabbage-based chowchow has a more pronounced sour taste. They also seem to have different origins, with piccalilli probably being a descendant of the pickled relishes, or atjars, of India.

In this version of this now-classic American relish, I have added a bit of clove and cinnamon to pep up the mixture a bit. As with chowchow, a jar of this colorful relish makes an excellent present, whatever the occasion.

Method: Rub the tomato slices with the salt and allow to stand overnight, covered and refrigerated. In the morning, squeeze the tomato slices between layers of cheesecloth to remove excess moisture, then set aside.

In a large saucepan, combine the vinegar, sugar, cloves, and cinnamon, and bring to a boil. Remove from the heat, add the reserved tomatoes, and stir well. Add the remaining ingredients and mix together well.

This piccalilli will keep, covered and refrigerated, several weeks.

5 green tomatoes about the size of baseballs, thinly sliced

2 tablespoons salt

2 cups white vinegar

2 cups sugar

1/2 teaspoon whole cloves

1/2 teaspoon ground cinnamon

Kernels from 3 ears corn, uncooked

1/2 red bell pepper, diced small

1/2 green bell pepper, diced small

1 red onion, diced small

FRESH CUCUMBER KIMCHI SALAD

Fresh Cucumber Kimchi Salad

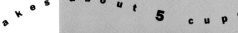

In this recipe, I have substituted cucumbers for the cabbage that forms the base of the most traditional form of Korean kimchi, and have added a few other vegetables as well. The result is a dish that is less pungent than fermented kimchi but has a very similar taste. To me, it tastes best if you let it sit for an hour or two so the various flavors get better acquainted.

You can serve this dish either as a salad course or a condiment. As usual, I think this goes best with pork, because that's my favorite kind of meat. But, if you like somewhat spicy tastes, you'll find this a good accompaniment for just about anything, from rice to fish to beef. Think of it as you would a dill pickle.

Method: Rub the cucumbers, carrots, and strips of bell pepper all over with the salt and allow to stand, covered and refrigerated, for 2 hours. Rinse *very* well and drain.

In a large bowl, combine the salted vegetables with all the remaining ingredients and mix well.

This kimchi salad will keep, covered and refrigerated, about 6 days.

3 unpeeled cucumbers, cut into thirds, then into finger-sized pieces

1 carrot, peeled and cut into finger-sized pieces

1 red bell pepper, cut into thin strips

½ cup salt

1 bunch watercress, well washed and trimmed of stems

1 tablespoon minced garlic

1 tablespoon minced fresh ginger

2 tablespoons sugar

¼ cup white vinegar

3 tablespoons paprika

1 tablespoon minced red or green chile pepper of your choice

2 tablespoons sesame seeds, toasted in a 350°F oven for 5 minutes

1 teaspoon crushed white pepper

PICKLED GRAPES WITH GINGER AND CHILES AND
CHICKEN PIECES ON THE GRILL

PICKLED GRAPES WITH GINGER AND CHILES

●

I have always felt a little uneasy using grapes in recipes. Maybe that is because, as a child, I related to this fruit most directly as the prime ingredient in the grape jelly I ate on my morning toast. But with age and a greater perspective, I've overcome my former apprehension.

These lightly pickled grapes, which keep their firm texture for months in the refrigerator, make a great accompaniment to baked ham, turkey, or any other roasted or grilled meat or fowl. If you use a mixture of red and green grapes, the colorful result also makes a good holiday gift.

Method: In a large saucepan, combine the white and brown sugar, vinegar, coriander seeds, cinnamon, cloves, and salt, mix well, and bring to a boil over moderately high heat. Remove from heat, add the ginger, jalapeño peppers, and grapes, mix thoroughly, and allow to stand 1 hour.

These grapes will keep, covered and refrigerated, almost indefinitely.

1 cup white sugar

½ cup brown sugar

1½ cups white vinegar

2 tablespoons crushed coriander seeds

1 tablespoon ground cinnamon

7 whole cloves

1 teaspoon salt

Piece of ginger the size of your little finger, peeled and sliced into slices about the thickness of a dime

3 red or green jalapeño peppers, thinly diced, seeds in

3 cups red and/or green seedless grapes

CUCUMBER CHOWCHOW WITH ROAST HAM

Cucumber Chowchow

Here's another version of chowchow, in which we stray from tradition a bit by featuring cucumbers. On the other hand, we stay closer here to the traditional method of preserving in heavy salt. I like the salty undertaste that is created by this process, but be sure to rinse the vegetables very well at the midpoint, or you will find yourself with too much of a good thing.

This chowchow is an excellent accompaniment to ham, turkey, or fried chicken—all those good Southern things.

Method: In a large bowl, combine all the vegetables, the garlic, and the kosher salt, and mix very well. Cover this mixture and let it sit in the refrigerator at least 6 hours or overnight.

Transfer the mixture to a colander, rinse very well several times, and set aside to drain.

Combine all the remaining ingredients in a large saucepan and bring to a boil, stirring constantly. Remove from the heat, add the drained vegetables, and allow to come to room temperature.

You may serve the chowchow at once, but the mixture will also keep, covered and refrigerated, up to 1 month.

2 unpeeled cucumbers, cut in half lengthwise, then thinly sliced

1 cup corn kernels (about 2 ears)

1 cup shredded green cabbage

1 red bell pepper, diced small

1 green bell pepper, diced small

1 red onion, thinly sliced

4 cloves garlic, peeled and thinly sliced

1/4 cup kosher salt

1 1/2 cups sugar

1 cup cider vinegar

2 tablespoons each dried mustard, mustard seeds, and celery seeds

1 teaspoon whole cloves

1 tablespoon freshly cracked black pepper

CHOWCHOW HOUND?

The name of this particular relish is a great example of the linguistic confusion that exists around common foods. Some experts say that "chowchow" derives from the Chinese word for "mixture," while others say it comes from the word for "dog," which seems particularly odd.

Wherever it originated, by modern times the name had come to mean very different things in different countries. The recipe for this chowchow will be recognized as chowchow by most Americans—and certainly by every Southerner. In a West Indian cookbook from the early 1940s, however, chowchow appears as a simple mixture of sliced mangoes, salt and pepper, and vinegar.

KOREA'S LITTLE DISHES

Kimchi is the generic name given to the fermented vegetable dishes of Korea. While kimchi is certainly central to Korean cuisine, it is only one part of the Korean tradition of "little dishes" known as *panchan.* This term, which may be loosely translated as "accompanying dishes," encompasses a wide range of preparations that are set out on the table to provide spice and variety to the rice, the central staple of any Korean meal. Another variation on the theme we're playing on in this book, *panchan* may include anything from pickled cucumbers to a peppery mixture of dried squid to a sweet-sour mixture based on fried anchovies.

RELISHES

A RELISH BY ANY OTHER NAME

•

If you have read the other parts of this book, you might be saying to yourself, "Wait a minute. All of this stuff seems the same to me, and couldn't you make it a lot easier by calling them *all* relishes?" Good point. You have achieved the zen of salsa and are now at one with the little dishes of intense flavor.

In fact, this is the catchall chapter. Here you'll find all the recipes that have the necessary pedigree or characteristics to be included in this book, but that for one arcane reason or another didn't work in the other categories.

We also wanted to encourage everyone to take seriously the point that labels are not important. All of the "little dishes" in this book are basically variations on the same, worldwide theme, and the key to their character is not their name, but the fact that all are easy to make and good for you, and taste great.

When you consider that the Indian word for "chutney" comes from the word for "relish," and that *"salsa"* translates as "sauce," it is clear that anyone setting sail in search of precise definition will soon find the waters of confusion closing over his or her head. Because of this, you might want to adopt this maxim: "If you don't know what it is, call it a relish. You may not be precise, but chances are you won't be wrong."

So let's just say that these are "little dishes" that add relish to any meal or snack, and leave it at that.

Since every country has some form of relish, in this chapter we serve up a real mixed bag, with something for everyone. Caribbean flavors predominate in Mango-Jicama Relish with Scotch Bonnet Peppers (page 95), for example, while Pampas Parsley-Onion Relish for Meat (page 101) is a variation on a traditional

Brazilian theme, and Tomato-Cucumber Relish with Lemon and Seeds (page 111) draws its inspiration from the Maharashtra state in India. If you have a serious addiction to Italian food, check out Peppered Oven-dried Tomato Relish (page 107), or Grilled Onion Relish with Black Olives and Basil (page 113). Whatever flavors you favor, there's a relish somewhere that will fill the bill.

MANGO-JICAMA RELISH WITH SCOTCH BONNET
PEPPERS AND TUNA STEAKS ON THE GRILL

MANGO-JICAMA RELISH WITH SCOTCH BONNET PEPPERS

•

Here's a relish that combines a range of truly great tastes—the lush, mellow sweetness of mangoes, the crisp juiciness of jicama, and the head-busting, floral heat of Scotch Bonnets, aka habanero peppers. Talk about "full-flavored"—this could be the dish they use to illustrate the term.

You will get a better texture to this dish if, when grating the jicama and the carrot, you drag them slowly along the grater so they come out in longish strips instead of little chips.

Try this one with your heavier-flavored grilled fish, like blue-fish, tuna, or mackerel.

Method: In a medium-sized bowl, mix all the ingredients together well.

This relish will keep, covered and refrigerated, 4 to 6 days.

1 jicama the size of a softball,* peeled and finely grated

1 carrot, peeled and finely grated

1 medium red onion, thinly sliced

2 ripe mangoes, peeled and diced small

2 cups mango juice (you may substitute pineapple juice)

¼ cup minced garlic

½ cup chopped fresh cilantro

8 scallions, top and bottom ½-inch trimmed off, then thinly sliced

2 tablespoons ground coriander

1 tablespoon ground cumin

2 fresh habanero peppers, split, seeded, and minced (you may substitute 2 tablespoons habanera-based hot sauce; Inner Beauty is the best, of course)

½ cup lime juice (about 4 limes)

Salt and freshly cracked black pepper to taste

*For you readers from Chicago, we mean a normal, regulation American softball. What's with that ball you use, anyway?

SPICY CUCUMBER-WATERMELON RELISH WITH
GRILLED HALF LOBSTER

SPICY CUCUMBER-WATERMELON RELISH

•

This is a variation on the classic cucumber relish that is omnipresent in the cuisines of Southeast Asia. Various versions of this simple, spicy relish appear in restaurants, street stalls, and homes throughout the region, but none contains watermelon—or at least none that I've seen. But I think it works, and it is truly international because guess what the Number One most popular fruit in the world is? That's right, watermelon.

This is a good relish with grilled shellfish of any variety.

Method: In a large bowl, mix all the ingredients together well.

This relish will keep, covered and refrigerated, 4 to 5 days.

2 unpeeled cucumbers, washed, halved, and thinly sliced

1 cup watermelon chunks the size of playing dice, seeded

½ small red onion, thinly sliced

1 carrot, peeled and thinly sliced

¼ cup rice wine vinegar (you may substitute white vinegar)

¼ cup sugar

1 teaspoon red pepper flakes

1 tablespoon chopped fresh mint

1 tablespoon chopped cilantro

Salt and freshly cracked white pepper to taste

RED ONION RELISH IN THE LATIN STYLE AND
GRILLED VEGETABLES

Cebollas Rojas Estilo Latino

RED ONION RELISH

IN THE LATIN STYLE

•

This simple relish features the flavors of Latin America. With the combination of raw onion, jalapeño pepper, and chili powder, it packs a decent wallop but is still mild enough for those folks who don't like anything *really* hot.

I like to serve this one with grilled pork chops and that Latin classic, black beans and rice. It's also good as an accompaniment to a big platter of roasted vegetables.

Method: In a medium-sized bowl, combine all the ingredients and mix well.

This relish will keep, covered and refrigerated, up to a week.

2 red onions, diced small

1 teaspoon minced garlic

5 tablespoons lime juice (about 2½ limes)

1 jalapeño pepper, chopped (you may substitute 1 teaspoon dried red pepper flakes)

1 teaspoon ground cumin

1 teaspoon chili powder

Salt and freshly cracked black pepper to taste

2 tablespoons chopped cilantro

PAMPAS PARSLEY-ONION RELISH WITH SLICED
NEW YORK STRIP STEAK

PAMPAS PARSLEY-ONION RELISH FOR MEAT

1 **bunch curly parsley, well washed and finely chopped**

1 **red onion, diced small**

1 **tablespoon minced red or green chile pepper of your choice**

1 **tablespoon minced garlic**

½ **cup virgin olive oil**

½ **cup lemon juice (about 2 lemons)**

This recipe is from my pal and former sous-chef Dr. Joey Knauss, who owns a great Brazilian restaurant named Pampas in Cambridge, Massachusetts. At his restaurant, Joey follows the Brazilian tradition of *charrascurria,* in which servers come around to your table with a seemingly endless variety of grilled meat and fowl on long skewers and slice off whatever amount each individual wants. To accompany this carnivore's fantasy come true, they serve this version of a traditional Brazilian relish.

Needless to say, this goes best with grilled meats, and particularly when you are grilling strong-flavored items like livers or hearts.

Method: In a medium-sized bowl, combine all the ingredients and mix well.

This relish will keep, covered and refrigerated, about 3 days.

GREEN APPLE–CHIPOTLE RELISH WITH GRILLED
BREAST OF CHICKEN

GREEN APPLE–CHIPOTLE RELISH

Makes about 4 cups

I have always liked the combination of the hot, smoky taste of chipotle peppers and the flavors of fruits. This particular combo was put together by our sous-chef at the East Coast Grill, Andrew Husbands. Here he joins chipotles with slightly tart Granny Smith apples, then adds the sweetness and acidity of oranges. This creates a very dynamic play of flavors, which work together best if you give them a few hours to get better acquainted after you have introduced them.

Andrew insists that this goes best with roast or grilled chicken. You might want to try it that way.

Method: In a large sauté pan, heat the vegetable oil over medium-high heat until hot but not smoking, add the onion, and cook for 2 minutes. Add the apples, cover, and continue to cook over medium heat, stirring occasionally, for an additional 8 minutes, or until the apples are a bit soft. Remove from the heat and set aside to cool.

Meanwhile, combine the chipotle, vinegar, and lemon juice in a blender or food processor and purée. Transfer to a medium-sized bowl, add the cumin, orange juice, oregano, and salt and pepper to taste, and mix well.

Add the orange, apples, and onions to the chipotle mixture and stir well. Allow to sit in refrigerator, covered, overnight or for at least 2 hours.

This relish will keep, covered and refrigerated, 7 to 10 days.

2 tablespoons vegetable oil

1 small onion

3 Granny Smith apples, cored and chopped into bite-sized pieces, peel left on

2 tablespoons minced chipotle peppers (see Pantry, page 133)

1½ teaspoons white vinegar

1½ teaspoons lemon juice (about ½ lemon)

1 teaspoon ground cumin

¼ cup orange juice

1 teaspoon chopped fresh oregano

Salt and freshly cracked black pepper to taste

1 orange, peeled, separated into segments, and roughly chopped

ORANGE-CUCUMBER RELISH WITH CHILE PEPPERS
AND MINT AND GRILLED TUNA STEAK

ORANGE-CUCUMBER RELISH WITH CHILE PEPPERS AND MINT

Makes about 3 cups

This colorful, refreshing relish combines several of the characteristic ingredients of Moroccan cooking and provides an excellent demonstration of the traditional flavors of North Africa. We find that the chile peppers add a pleasing bite to the sweetness of the oranges and the smooth coolness of the cucumbers. Don't use dried mint in this recipe, as it has a powdery texture that really doesn't work well. If fresh mint is not available, substitute some other fresh herb, such as cilantro, basil, or marjoram, all of which are also used occasionally in Moroccan cuisine.

Try this one with fish; we particularly like it with rich fish like tuna, mackerel, or bluefish.

Method: In a medium-sized mixing bowl, combine all the ingredients and mix well.

This relish will keep, covered and refrigerated, 2 to 3 days.

3 navel oranges, peeled, seeded, and chopped into bite-sized pieces

2 small cucumbers, peeled, cut in half lengthwise, and sliced into ¼-inch slices

½ red onion, halved and thinly sliced

2 tablespoons vegetable oil

¼ cup red wine vinegar

¼ cup orange juice

2 teaspoons minced red or green chile pepper of your choice

2 tablespoons finely chopped fresh mint

Salt and freshly cracked black pepper to taste

PEPPERED OVEN-DRIED TOMATO RELISH WITH
ENDIVE AND STEAMED ASPARAGUS

PEPPERED OVEN-DRIED TOMATO RELISH

Makes about 4 cups

•

Mediterranean cooks have been drying tomatoes in the sun for hundreds of years. As with other fruits, the drying concentrates the flavor and the sweetness of the tomatoes. Here we approximate the sun-drying process by drying tomatoes in the oven, after first giving them a heavy coat of freshly cracked black pepper. When combined with other Mediterranean flavors—basil, capers, and balsamic vinegar—the result is a relish that is simultaneously sweet, tart, and spicy.

This makes a great spread or dip for bread, crackers, or crudités as part of an antipasto. Or try putting it on croutons and adding them to a salad.

Method : In a small bowl, combine all the pepper rub ingredients, then rub this mixture onto the cut surfaces of the tomatoes. Arrange the tomato halves in a single layer on top of a rack placed on a large baking tray or sheet pan, and slow-bake in a 190°F oven overnight, or about 8 hours. As they cook, the tomatoes will become wrinkled and shrunken; smaller ones will slip through the rack and end up on the baking tray. After 8 hours, remove the tomatoes and set them aside to cool.

When the tomatoes are at room temperature, chop them roughly and place them in a large bowl. Add all the remaining ingredients and mix well.

This relish will keep, covered and refrigerated, several weeks.

10 baseball-sized ripe tomatoes, stemmed and halved

THE PEPPER RUB

¼ cup virgin olive oil

¼ cup freshly cracked black pepper

2 tablespoons coarse salt

1 tablespoon minced garlic

THE RELISH

1 red onion, diced small

¼ cup finely chopped fresh basil

¼ cup large capers

¼ cup virgin olive oil

¼ cup balsamic vinegar

Salt and freshly cracked black pepper to taste

SWEET AND SPICY PEACH RELISH OVER GRILLED
SWORDFISH STEAK

Sweet and Spicy Peach Relish

Peaches are a great fruit for relishes. I love their color, their flavor, and the way they blend so easily with the other tastes of hot-weather climates. For this Caribbean-inspired version, I recommend you use peaches that are somewhere between green and dead-ripe—that is, ripe enough to have flavor, but not so ripe that they lose their shape when mixed with the other ingredients.

Whether you're grilling fish or roasting a pork loin, this relish is a great accompaniment. Try it, for example, with grilled swordfish or kingfish.

Method: In a large bowl, combine all the ingredients and mix well.

This relish will keep, covered and refrigerated, about 4 days.

4 large ripe or semiripe peaches, pitted and thinly sliced

1 red bell pepper, cut into thin strips

1 green bell pepper, cut into thin strips

1 red onion, peeled and very thinly sliced

½ cup orange juice

¼ cup virgin olive oil

6 tablespoons lime juice (about 3 limes)

1 tablespoon molasses

1 tablespoon minced red or green chile pepper of your choice

½ cup chopped Italian or curly parsley

1 teaspoon minced garlic

Salt and freshly cracked black pepper to taste

TOMATO-CUCUMBER RELISH WITH LEMON AND
SEEDS OVER RICE PILAF

Tomato-Cucumber Relish with Lemon and Seeds

This relish is modeled after koshimbirs, the everyday relishes of India's Maharashtra state that Madhur Jaffrey describes so well in *A Taste of India* (Atheneum).

With its strong lemon taste, this relish goes well with any kind of fish, but it is also great for spooning over steamed vegetables or rice—it will certainly add a hefty jolt of intense flavor.

Method: In a large bowl, combine all the ingredients and mix well.

This relish will keep, covered and refrigerated, about 4 days.

- 1 baseball-sized tomato, diced small
- 1 unpeeled cucumber, seeds in, diced small
- 1 small red onion, diced small
- 1 teaspoon minced red or green chile pepper of your choice
- ¾ cup lemon juice (about 3 lemons)
- 1 tablespoon sugar
- 1 teaspoon each crushed cumin seeds, crushed coriander seeds, black mustard seeds (you may substitute yellow seeds)
- Salt and freshly cracked black pepper to taste

GRILLED ONION RELISH WITH BLACK OLIVES AND
BASIL OVER FETTUCCINE

GRILLED ONION RELISH WITH BLACK OLIVES AND BASIL

•

I love the sweet, slightly charred taste of grilled onions. Here they are combined with the loamy taste of cured black olives, fresh basil, and garlic to create a relish that features strong Mediterranean flavors. To add just a bit of bite, I have thrown in a couple shots of Tabasco sauce. To my mind, some Italian foods call for heat.

If you are a beef fancier, this relish is ideal for a big, juicy, peppered grilled steak. It's also great with leftover cold pasta.

Method: Rub the onion halves well with the olive oil and sprinkle with salt and freshly cracked pepper. Grill over a medium-hot fire. To check the fire temperature, hold your hand about 5 inches above the grilling surface. If you can hold it there for 1 to 2 seconds, you have a hot fire; 3 to 4 seconds, a medium fire; and 5 to 6 seconds, a low fire. Longer than that, and your fire is too cool. Grill the onion halves until golden brown, about 3 to 4 minutes per side. Remove them from the grill, allow to cool, and chop roughly.

In a large mixing bowl, combine the grilled onions with all the remaining ingredients and mix well.

This relish will keep, covered and refrigerated, 4 to 5 days.

3 large onions, peeled and halved

3 tablespoons virgin olive oil

Salt and freshly cracked black pepper to taste

¼ cup pitted cured black olives, Kalamata or another variety, roughly chopped

¼ cup fresh basil, cut into long, thin strips

1 tablespoon minced garlic

¼ cup balsamic vinegar

¼ cup lemon juice (about 1 lemon)

¼ cup virgin olive oil

2 shots Tabasco sauce

MEDITERRANEAN ROASTED CORN AND PEPPER
RELISH OVER MIXED GREENS

MEDITERRANEAN ROASTED CORN AND PEPPER RELISH

•

Smoky corn mixed with smoky peppers and the spirited bite of citrus—this is a super relish for the summertime. It goes great with grilled fish or served on toast as a first course. I also like it mixed with crisp lettuce as an unusual summer salad, or in last night's leftover plain pasta.

Method: Rub the corn lightly with the vegetable oil and sprinkle with salt and freshly cracked pepper. Grill the corn over a low fire. To check the fire temperature, hold your hand about 5 inches above the grilling surface. If you can hold it there for 1 to 2 seconds, you have a hot fire; 3 to 4 seconds, a medium fire; and 5 to 6 seconds, a low fire. Longer than that, and your fire is too cool. Roll the ears around with your tongs to be sure they cook evenly, until the corn is slightly charred, about 7 to 10 minutes. Remove the ears from the grill and, as soon as they are cool enough to handle, slice the kernels off the cobs. In a large bowl, mix the kernels together with all the remaining ingredients.

This relish will keep, covered and refrigerated, 4 to 5 days.

3 ears corn, husked and desilked

1 tablespoon vegetable oil

Salt and freshly cracked black pepper to taste

3 roasted red bell peppers (see Pantry, page 145), cut into thin slices

¼ cup chopped parsley

2 teaspoons minced garlic

¼ cup virgin olive oil

¼ cup lemon juice (about 1 lemon)

CATSUPS AND OTHER CONDIMENTS

LAY IT ON THICK

•

Just to give you an idea or two, I recently read an old American cookbook that included catsups made from cucumbers, cranberries, onions, grapes, lemons, and apples, along with combinations like tomatoes and red wine or cucumbers and black pepper.

I have also included here a recipe for a pungent, flavorful mustard that combines apricots and coriander with the standard mustard seeds, and a sweet onion spread that features Mediterranean flavors. The way I see it, the more condiments you have to spread, the better.

Today, most of us think of catsup only as the tomato-based sauce that appears in bottles on every diner counter, restaurant table, and dining room table in America. We would never denigrate this classic condiment, and when it comes to hamburgers or french fries there is nothing that can beat it. But it is only over the past hundred years or so that "catsup" has come to mean just this one sauce.

Although there is (naturally) some disagreement about its exact pedigree, everyone allows that what we now know as catsup originated somewhere in Asia as a salty, fish-based sauce. If you try to trace it by linguistics, however, you can't get too precise—you have your choice of *ketsiap* from China, *kechap* from Malaysia, or *ketjap* from Indonesia.

In any case, catsup arrived in Europe sometime in the seventeenth century and quickly took on some of its present character. Since fish brine was not a common ingredient there, European versions of this condiment were based on vinegar and spices and contained a wide range of ingredients in place of the standard tomato we think of today. Making catsup out of something was thought of primarily as a way of preserving that product, and home cooks and chefs alike made catsups of everything from mushrooms to walnuts to horseradish root.

Here we have given you recipes for catsups made from mushrooms, papayas, and peaches, which gives you a real range of flavors. If you feel like it, go ahead and create your own catsups. The basic idea is that this is a vinegar-based, spicy condiment with a vegetable or fruit as a main ingredient. Go wild.

STAN'S PEACH CATSUP WITH DEEP-FRIED VIDALIA ONIONS

STAN'S PEACH CATSUP

This is a great way to use slightly overripe peaches; when they start to develop a few little brown spots, just toss 'em into a catsup. Their flavor is truly incredible at that point. Of course, you can also use just regular ripe peaches too.

This recipe is from my friend and business partner, Stan Frankenthaler, chef at The Blue Room in Cambridge, Massachusetts, and a good ol' boy from Georgia. Here you can see the intersection of a modern chef and his culinary roots.

Since this is a Southern-inspired recipe, try it with any type of chicken, particularly barbecued or fried. Or, if you want to be really right, serve it with a batch of french-fried Vidalia onions.

Method: In a saucepot, heat the oil over high heat until hot but not smoking. Sauté the onion slices in the vegetable oil over medium heat until transparent, about 5 minutes. Add the peaches and cook for an additional 4 minutes, stirring frequently. Add all the remaining ingredients except the lemon juice and simmer over low heat for 1 hour, stirring occasionally. If necessary, add a small amount of water to prevent the mixture from burning.

Remove from the heat, add the lemon juice, and purée in a blender or food processor.

This catsup will keep, covered and refrigerated, several weeks.

1 **tablespoon vegetable oil**

1 **large onion, thinly sliced**

5 **ripe peaches, pitted and roughly chopped**

¼ **cup brown sugar, packed**

3 **tablespoons molasses**

2 **tablespoons white sugar**

1 **teaspoon salt**

½ **teaspoon freshly cracked black pepper**

¼ **teaspoon ground allspice**

½ **cup white vinegar**

2 **tablespoons lemon juice (about ½ lemon)**

SMOKY SHIITAKE MUSHROOM CATSUP

SMOKY SHIITAKE MUSHROOM CATSUP

Makes about 2 cups

1 pound shiitake mushrooms, bottom half of the stems removed

1 onion, peeled and quartered

2 tablespoons virgin olive oil

Salt and freshly cracked black pepper to taste

¼ cup balsamic vinegar

1 teaspoon minced garlic

1 tablespoon molasses

2 tablespoons chopped fresh basil

Shiitakes are great on the grill—they are big, so they're easy to grill; they pick up the smoky taste like a sponge; and they also take on a nice sear. Be sure to grill up a couple of extra ones, because you will definitely want to munch on a few before you purée the rest with the other catsup ingredients.

Although some people think that it's déclassé to put catsup on a steak, here's a chance to beat those snobs at their own game.

Method: Rub the mushrooms and onions with the olive oil and grill over a hot fire. To check the fire temperature, hold your hand about 5 inches above the grilling surface. If you can hold it there for 1 to 2 seconds, you have a hot fire; 3 to 4 seconds, a medium fire; and 5 to 6 seconds, a low fire. Longer than that, and your fire is too cool. Grill the mushrooms 2 to 3 minutes per side, or until they get floppy. Roll the onions around on the grill so they get charred on all sides, about 7 minutes total cooking time. Remove them from the grill.

Put the mushrooms, onions, and all the remaining ingredients in a food processor or blender and purée. Adjust seasoning.

This catsup will keep, covered and refrigerated, 4 to 5 days, but is best served warm.

CHUNKY PAPAYA CATSUP ON A GRILLED HAMBURGER

Chunky Papaya Catsup

This tropical-flavored catsup uses the Indian technique of frying spices before using them. This seems to intensify the flavors of the spices, makes them easier to digest, and sure makes your kitchen aromatic.

Basically, this is a smooth chutney, with the sweet-sour taste contrasts characteristic of the genre, and lends itself to many combinations. It's great on a burger or as a basting sauce or with horseradish as a tropical cocktail sauce. Or try it on deep fried plantain chips.

Method: In a large sauté pan, heat the vegetable oil over medium heat until hot but not smoking. Add the onions and sauté about 5 to 7 minutes, stirring frequently, until onions have become translucent and have begun to char slightly. Add the bell peppers and cook an additional 2 minutes, stirring frequently. Add the garlic and spices and cook an additional 2 minutes, stirring constantly. The mixture will be quite dry at this point.

Add the papaya, vinegar, pineapple juice, and molasses, stir well, and allow to come to a boil. Reduce the heat to low and simmer for about 25 minutes, or until the mixture has become slightly thinner than tomato catsup. (It will thicken up more as it cools.) Add the lemon juice, salt and pepper to taste, and stir well.

This catsup will keep, covered and refrigerated, 3 to 4 days.

4 tablespoons vegetable oil

1 onion, peeled and diced small

1/2 red bell pepper, diced small

1/2 green bell pepper, diced small

1 teaspoon minced garlic

1 tablespoon each ground allspice, curry powder, and ground cumin

4 ripe papayas, peeled, seeded, and cut into bite-sized chunks

1 cup white vinegar

1 cup pineapple juice

1/2 cup molasses

2 tablespoons lemon juice (about 1/2 lemon)

Salt and freshly cracked black pepper to taste

SWEET RED ONION–GARLIC SPREAD ON CRUSTY
BREAD WITH MINESTRONE

SWEET RED ONION-GARLIC SPREAD

Makes about 2 cups

•

4 red onions, peeled, halved, and thinly sliced

7 tablespoons virgin olive oil

4 whole heads of garlic

1 tablespoon balsamic vinegar

5 tablespoons chopped fresh thyme

Salt and freshly cracked black pepper to taste

Red onions start out milder than other onions to begin with, and, to me, long sautéing seems to concentrate their sweetness. In this condimentlike spread, I combine them with garlic, another root that becomes mellower and sweeter with cooking. The result is a spread with great sweetness and resonant, earthy flavors.

If I'm having a hearty soup, I'll be making some of this to spread on crusty bread to go with it.

Method: Cook the onions with 3 tablespoons of the olive oil over medium heat in a large sauté pan, stirring constantly after the first 5 minutes, until the onions become brownish and slightly gooey. This will take about 15 to 20 minutes. Remove them from the heat and set aside.

Meanwhile, wrap the unpeeled heads of garlic in tinfoil along with the remaining 4 tablespoons of olive oil, and roast them in a 350°F oven for 45 minutes. Remove them and allow to cool to room temperature.

When the garlic heads are cool, squeeze the meat from the cloves and combine it with the cooked onions. (I find it works best to squeeze the cloves from the tip toward the base.) Add the balsamic vinegar, thyme, and salt and pepper to taste, and purée the mixture in a food processor or blender.

This spread will keep, covered and refrigerated, several weeks.

COARSE-GRAIN APRICOT MUSTARD WITH CORN
BEEF ON RYE

COARSE-GRAIN APRICOT MUSTARD

●

1 cup black mustard seeds (or you may substitute yellow seeds)

3 tablespoons dry powdered mustard

1 cup water

½ cup cider vinegar

½ cup orange juice

½ cup dried apricots, diced small

2 tablespoons coriander seeds, crushed

Salt and freshly cracked black pepper to taste

'm always curious about how everyday stuff, the things we have been eating since we were kids, gets made. In the case of mustard, mustard seeds are ground into a powder and mixed with liquids and other spices to make the paste we are familiar with, which has been around in one form or another since the days of the Roman Empire.

In this version of the venerable condiment, we leave the mustard grainy to add texture, and stir in apricots and coriander seeds to provide some interesting complementary flavors. The result is a pretty biting affair, but it will mellow over time, so we recommend that you let it sit in the refrigerator, covered, for several days before you use it.

We prefer black mustard seeds because they are somewhat less pungent but still as flavorful, and I like the resulting color better. You may substitute the more common yellow seeds.

This mustard is wonderful when spread over cold meat sandwiches, particularly roast beef, corned beef, or cold pork.

Method: Grind the mustard seeds in a spice mill or coffee grinder until they are the texture of coarse cornmeal. Transfer to a medium-sized bowl. Add the powdered mustard, water, vinegar, and orange juice, and stir well. Allow this mixture to stand for 2 hours, then stir again.

Add the apricots, coriander seeds, and salt and freshly cracked pepper to taste, and mix again.

The mustard will keep, covered and refrigerated, 2 to 3 weeks.

PANTRY

•

Black Beans: Also known as "turtle beans," these smooth-surfaced little legumes are a fixture of South and Central American cuisines, particularly in Mexico, Cuba, and Brazil. They are available canned or dried in the "ethnic foods" sections of most U.S. supermarkets. The canned variety are perfectly acceptable, but are a bit mushy for my taste and don't have the full flavor of dried ones cooked with the following recipe:

Your Basic Black Beans: Soak 2 cups dried black beans in cold water to cover overnight or for at least 5 hours, then drain and rinse well. In a large saucepan, heat 3 tablespoons peanut oil until hot but not smoking, then add 2 large yellow onions, diced, and sauté over high heat until clear, 4 to 5 minutes. Add 2 tablespoons minced garlic and sauté another minute, then add 1 teaspoon each of chili powder, ground cumin, Tabasco sauce, and sugar, along with ¼ cup white vinegar, 2 cups water, the beans, and a bottle of your favorite beer. Bring to a simmer, cover well, and cook over low heat for 3 hours or until the beans are soft to the bite. Don't overcook or the beans will become mushy.

chiles: These fiery little pods, members of the capsicum family, are worthy of many books in their own right. After their "discovery" by the Europeans who came to the Americas in the fifteenth century, chiles spread around the globe, becoming inextricably entwined in the cuisines of many countries. To us, they are indispensable ingredients.

Since there are over two thousand varieties of chiles, each with its own heat level and individual flavor, we will make no attempt to catalogue them all here. In fact, you will notice that, when we call for chiles in a recipe, we generally refrain from specifying which variety you should use. Instead, we call for a certain amount of "red or green chile pepper of your choice." This is because we think it is most rewarding to locate a

particular variety of chile that you enjoy and that is readily available in your area, then develop a relationship with it. That way you will get to know just how hot a dish will be if you add "x" amount of your favorite chile. There are, however, a couple of chiles whose taste and heat are so distinctive that they really should be used when specifically called for in a recipe. We consider the chipotle and the habanero in this category and have included them as separate entries here.

While we're on that subject, let's add the obvious: Only you know how hot you like your food, so only you will know how much of your favorite pepper to include in any given recipe. Our suggested amount is just that—a suggestion, not a rule.

This is the name given to the dried, smoked jalapeño pepper. It has a unique, smoky, imposing flavor that goes with everything, and (particularly important for novice chile users) a consistent level of heat. It usually comes canned, packed in an *adobo* sauce, a mixture of onions, tomatoes, vinegar, and spices. However, it is also found dried. To use the dried variety, place in very hot water and allow to soak for 40 minutes to reconstitute. In a real pinch, you may substitute a mixture of 1 puréed fresh pepper of your choice, 1 teaspoon catsup, and 1 drop Liquid Smoke for each chipotle called for. The chipotle is flat and wrinkled, with a dark reddish-brown color, and about 1 to 1½ inches long.

CLOCKWISE FROM LEFT: JALAPEÑO, CANNED CHIPOTLE IN ADOBE SAUCE, AND DRIED CHIPOTLE

cilantro: Also known as fresh coriander, Mexican parsley, or Asian parsley, this pungent, highly aromatic herb is central to the cooking of Mexico, Latin America, and Southeast Asia. Almost unknown to Americans a mere decade ago, it is now widely available. The taste of cilantro is very distinct, and some people compare it to the flavor of soap or stainless steel. We never felt that way, and most of the people we know who originally reacted that way have ended up acquiring a taste for it. However, if you really detest the taste, you can substitute fresh parsley. We prefer to use it raw, adding it to cooked dishes only at the last minute, since cooking greatly diminishes its flavor. Drying also largely destroys its aromatic nature, so we would urge you to make the effort to get the fresh herb.

Coriander Seeds: The coriander is a double-duty culinary plant. Like the leaves and stems (commonly known as cilantro), the seeds are also widely used in Asian and Latin cooking. Lightly toasted and ground to a powder, they are an essential ingredient in curry powders as well as many chutneys and sambals.

When we call for whole coriander seeds, we recommend that you toast them before using them, since this brings out their flavor and aroma. When ground coriander is called for, you can either use preground or you can toast the seeds and grind them yourself, again with a little better result.

To toast the seeds, heat a sauté pan over medium heat and place the seeds in it. Toast them, watching carefully and shaking frequently to avoid burning, until they just begin to release a little smoke, about 2 to 3 minutes. That's it. If the recipe calls for ground coriander, this is the point at which you grind them in a spice mill or coffee grinder. If you don't have either of those tools, you can easily crush the seeds with the bottom of the sauté pan you used to toast them.

you can toast the seeds and grind them yourself, again with a little better result.

To toast the seeds, heat a sauté pan over medium heat and place the seeds in it. Toast them, watching carefully and shaking frequently to avoid burning, until they just begin to release a little smoke, about 2 to 3 minutes. If the recipe calls for ground cumin, grind the toasted seeds in a spice mill or coffee grinder, or crush them with the bottom of a sauté pan.

C u m i n   S e e d s : These greenish-yellow seeds with their distinctive flavor are an integral part of the cooking of India, and are also used in Latin, African, and Middle Eastern cuisines. There is also a black variety of cumin, which has a sweeter, more refined, and more complex flavor, but it is expensive and difficult to locate.

As with coriander seeds, when we call for whole cumin seeds, we recommend that you toast them before using them to bring out their flavor and aroma. Similarly, when ground cumin is called for, you can either use pre-ground or

F i s h   S a u c e : What salt is to Western cooking, what soy sauce is to Chinese cuisine, fish sauce is to the cuisines of Southeast Asia. Known as *nuoc mam* in Vietnam, *nam pla* in Thailand, and *nam pa* in Laos, this thin, brownish sauce is made by packing anchovies or other small fish in salt and allowing them to ferment for three months or more, then drawing off the accumulated liquid. While the process may sound strange, the resulting sauce can quickly become addictive. When used properly, *nuoc mam,* like salt, does not stand out as an individual taste, but adds a real depth of flavor to any Southeast Asian dish.

In Vietnam, *nuoc mam* is the primary ingredient in the table sauce known as *nuoc cham,* served with most meals, for which a recipe is given on page 142.

Also known as the Scotch Bonnet in the Caribbean, the habanero is generally acknowledged as the hottest commercially available chile pepper in the world. This baby, with its Scoville heat rating of up to 300,000 (compared with the jalapeño's 2,500–5,000 Scoville units), will take you places you've never been before. It has a unique, floral flavor and an over-the-top nasal heat that is quite different from the flat, back-of-the-throat heat of many other chile peppers. Because of this, when a recipe specifically calls for habaneros, we recommend that you make a real effort to locate them rather than substituting other varieties.

These peppers sometimes show up unpredictably in various markets, and if you happen upon them, buy a bunch and freeze them for later use, which will not damage them or reduce their heat or flavor. If you can't find habaneros, you may substitute Inner Beauty Hot Sauce or any of the other habanero/Scotch Bonnet–based sauces, using about 1 tablespoon of sauce for each pepper called for in the recipe. The habanero is a short, fat, lantern-shaped pepper, about 1 to 1½ inches long and 1 inch in diameter, and may range in color from yellow to red-orange to green to white.

A word of caution: When working with habaneros, be sure to wear gloves, and if you get any of the juice on your skin, wash it off with a mild bleach solution, which neutralizes the capsaicin. Also, be sure you don't rub your eyes or other sensitive areas while working with these peppers, and wash your hands well after you're done. If you have ever failed to follow these precautions, you will know why we are stressing them.

Jalapeño Chile Pepper:

This is the best known and most widely consumed fresh chile pepper in the United States. It is easy to locate and, although relatively low on the heat scale of chile peppers, still packs a decent punch. It comes in both red and green varieties; although the red is a bit more difficult to locate, we find it has a richer flavor. You may also find jalapeños pickled (*en escabeche*). The jalapeño is plump and bullet-shaped, with a sleek and shiny exterior, about 1 to 1½ inches long.

CLOCKWISE FROM LEFT: JALAPEÑO, CANNED CHIPOTLE IN ADOBE SAUCE, AND DRIED CHIPOTLE

Jicama: This tuber, which has a crisp, crunchy texture and a sweetish taste that lies somewhere between an apple and a potato, originated in the southern hemisphere of the Americas. It was taken to the Philippines by the Spanish, and eventually spread throughout the Pacific Rim, where it is widely used today. In the United States, the jicama has become increasingly familiar over the past few years, as Latin and Asian ethnic cuisines have gained popularity, and can be found in many urban supermarkets. Peel its skin off with a knife, cover it with water, and jicama will keep, covered and refrigerated, for up to 2 days.

Kosher Salt: This coarse-grained sea salt containing natural iodine is the only type that we use. We particularly like it in relishes because it dissolves more quickly than iodized salt, and because to us it has a better flavor than the free-flowing variety. Besides, it's more fun to sprinkle this stuff on with your fingers than to shake the standard variety out of a shaker.

Mace: When you remove the green outer husk from a fresh nutmeg, the interior is a brilliant crimson red. The startling color is provided not by the nutmeg itself, however, but by the casing that surrounds it. When dried and ground to a powder, this casing is called mace. Highly aromatic and slightly milder in flavor than nutmeg, mace is a familiar spice in Southeast Asian and Caribbean cooking.

Mango : This luscious, fragrant fruit comes in as many different varieties as the apple does, and it is a daily staple in more than half of the world. Like the papaya, the mango is used as a vegetable in its green state—either cooked or

added raw to salads and relishes—and as a fruit in its ripe state. Due to the fruit's large pit and the slippery nature of the flesh, the flesh of the mango can be somewhat difficult to get at, but it is well worth the effort.

Mustard Seeds: Mustard seeds, one of the world's oldest spices, come in three varieties—black, brown, and yellow. Oddly enough, all are members of the cabbage family. The yellow variety, whose color is actually a kind of off-white, are the least flavorful of the three and the most common in American and European cooking. Black mustard seeds have a stronger, deeper flavor and are more commonly used in Asian and Indian cuisines. The brown variety, often lumped in with black, actually has a bit more bite. We like the black seeds best, but you can always substitute yellow or brown if they are more readily available.

Nuoc Cham: In Vietnam, this condiment is served with most meals. As with American barbecue sauce and Indian curries, each Vietnamese cook has their own version of *nuoc cham,* and here is mine:

For about 3 cups of *Nuoc Cham,* whisk together the following ingredients in a large bowl: ½ cup fish sauce, ¼ cup lime juice (about 2 limes), ½ cup sugar, 1 cup warm water, ¼ cup rice wine vinegar, 1 tablespoon red pepper flakes, 1 tablespoon shredded garlic, and ¼ cup grated carrots. This sauce will keep, covered and refrigerated, for about 2 months.

P a p a y a : Used as a vegetable when green and a fruit when ripe, the papaya is native to the Caribbean (where it is also known as the "paw paw") and is found in tropical regions throughout the world. The musky-flavored fruit ranges in color from greenish-yellow when underripe to bright orange or red when fully ripe. The papaya, which can grow up to twenty pounds in size, is used as a salad or salsa ingredient, cooked in soups, or eaten raw as a kind of snack food with just a squeeze of lime juice. Unfortunately, the papaya travels poorly, so most Americans have never had the opportunity to taste it at its peak. In urban areas, papayas are sold in Latin markets, specialty stores, and supermarkets.

Rice Wine Vinegar:
This is simply a vinegar made from fermented rice (duh!, as my ten-year-old nephew Tommy would say), which has a milder, less acidic taste than most other vinegars. It is usually used in conjunction with Asian dishes.

Quince: Once very popular in the United States as a preserved fruit, the quince is now a rarity in this country. Perhaps this is because it has an unusually dry texture for a fruit and does not develop much sugar even when completely ripe. These drawbacks are compensated for, however, by the distinctly tropical, musky perfume of this aromatic fruit.

Roasted Red Bell Peppers:

Roasting a bell pepper removes the skin and adds a rich, smoky flavor. It might seem like an odd technique at first, since it basically involves burning the exterior of the pepper, but after you taste the results you will be torching these babies every time the grill is out.

To roast beli peppers, put them on the grill over a hot fire and roll them around until the skin is completely dark and well blistered. Remove from the grill, pop into a brown paper bag, tie the bag shut, and allow the peppers to cool in the bag for about 1 hour. (This facilitates the removal of the skin.) After an hour, remove the peppers from the bag and sort of fondle them in your hands, caressing the skins into falling off. Tear the peppers in half, remove the inner cores and seeds, and run the peppers gently under cold water to remove any remaining charred pieces of skin. Put them into a small container, add virgin olive oil to cover, cover the container, and refrigerate. They will keep up to 2 weeks stored in this manner.

Shiitake Mushroom:
Perhaps the most popular of the "exotic" mushrooms, the shiitake has many attractive attributes, including large size, dense texture, and rich, loamy flavor. It lends itself particularly well to grilling. Until the last decade or so, fresh shiitakes were found only in Asia. These days, however, they are grown in the United States, and good specimens can be found in most specialty produce stores and many supermarkets in urban areas.

Shrimp Paste: It is hard to overemphasize the importance of this preparation in the cuisines of Southeast Asia, particularly in Malaysia and Indonesia, where it is virtually ubiquitous. Known as *belacan* in Malaysia, *mam tom* in Vietnam, *gapi* in Thailand, and *trasi* in Indonesia, this paste of fermented, dried shrimp or prawns is used rather sparingly in each individual dish, like salt or pepper in Western cooking.

Star Anise : With its eight-pointed, star-shaped pods and its strong licorice flavor, this seedpod of an Asian evergreen tree is one of the more exotic spices readily available to American cooks. It is an essential ingredient of the Chinese five-spice powder, and is frequently used in Vietnamese cooking as well as that of other Southeast Asian countries.

Tomatillo: This tart Latin American staple looks like a small, unripe tomato with a papery brown husk. It is cooked and used in sauces and salsas in Latin cuisine, and is widely available in the United States canned as well as fresh.

WHERE DO YOU GET THAT STUFF?

Most of the ingredients in this book can be found in supermarkets or produce markets around the country. However, some are a bit out of the ordinary and may take some searching. If you don't think that your town has a source for these slightly unusual ingredients, think again—if there are a few Chinese restaurants in town, or Mexican ones, or ones serving any other ethnic cuisine, chances are there is a local source for at least some of the ingredients they use in their cooking. Ask the chef; he or she will usually be glad to give you the information.

Also, if you have an immigrant group in your area, they certainly have markets where the foods of their home country are found. Small stores in ethnic neighborhoods often have ingredients not carried by large chains. With a little research, you can easily find the Latin or Chinese market in your area, for example. Going to these markets is more than just shopping for food, it is a window on other cultures, and adds a whole different dimension to cooking. To us, this is definitely superior to paying a sometimes phenomenal markup for the same items (and usually less variety) in your local upscale gourmet store.

In case there are some ingredients that you can't find in your locality, do not despair. These days, almost everything under the sun is available by mail order. Here are a few mail-order sources you might want to try. Many of them also have catalogues they will send you, which is fun because then you can browse through the pages of exotic foreign ingredients. If no particular regional specialty is noted for a source, that means it carries a wide range of hard-to-find ingredients.

ADRIANA'S BAZAAR
  (high-quality spices)
2152 Broadway
New York, NY 10023
(212) 877-5757

BALDUCCI'S
424 Sixth Avenue
New York, NY 10011
(800) 572-7041
In New York: (800) 225-3822

CMC COMPANY
  (Mexican/Latin ingredients)
P.O. Drawer B
Avalon, NJ 08202
(800) CMC-2780

DEAN & DELUCA
560 Broadway
New York, NY 10012
(800) 221-7714
In New York: (212) 431-1691

DEWILDT IMPORTS
  (Asian ingredients)
Fox Gap Road
R.D. 3
Bangor, PA 18013
(800) 338-3433

FRIEDA'S BY MAIL
  (Specialty and exotic produce)
P.O. Box 58488
Los Angeles, CA 90058
(800) 241-1771

G. B. RATTO, INTERNATIONAL GROCERS
821 Washington Street
Oakland, CA 94607
(800) 325-3483
In California: (800) 228-3515

K. KALUSTAN
  (Indian and Asian ingredients)
123 Lexington Avenue
New York, NY 10016
(212) 685-3451

LA PALMA
  (Latin/Caribbean ingredients)
2884 Twenty-fourth Street
San Francisco, CA 94110
(415) 647-1500

RAFAL SPICE COMPANY
2521 Russell Street
Detroit, MI 48207
(800) 228-4276

STAR MARKET
  (Asian ingredients)
3349 North Clark Street
Chicago, IL 60657
(312) 472-0599

SULTAN'S DELIGHT
  (Middle Eastern/North African ingredients)
P.O. Box 253
Staten Island, NY 10314
(800) 852-5046

TROPICANA MARKET
  (Latin ingredients)
5001 Lindenwood Street
St. Louis, MO 63109
(314) 353-7328

For Dried Chile Peppers:
LOS CHILEROS DE NUEVO MEXICO
P.O. Box 6215
Santa Fe, NM 87502
(505) 471-6967

For Inner Beauty Hot Sauce:
LE SAUCIER
Quincy Market, North Canopy
Boston, MA 02109
(617) 522-5446

OR

MO' HOTTA, MO' BETTA
P.O. Box 4136
San Luis Obispo, CA 93403
(800) 462-3220

INDEX

ABOUT THE
AUTHORS

•

Chris Schlesinger and John Willoughby are the co-authors of **The Thrill of the Grill** (Morrow, 1990). The short story is: These are two guys who like to cook food and drink beer with friends in places where the weather is hot. Then they write about it. Here's the long story:

Chris Schlesinger is the chef and co-owner of the East Coast Grill, Jake and Earl's Dixie Barbecue, and The Blue Room, all located in Cambridge, Massachusetts.

Chris was born and raised in Virginia, where he first developed his lifelong devotion to barbecue, spicy food, and live-fire cookery. He entered the food-service industry at the age of eighteen, when he dropped out of college to become a dishwasher. After graduating from the Culinary Institute of America in 1977, Chris cooked in over thirty restaurants, having the opportunity to work with some of the most innovative chefs in New England during the first blossoming of nouvelle cuisine. In 1986, he and partner Cary Wheaton opened the East Coast Grill, the first of their restaurants. This was followed by Jake and Earl's in 1989 and The Blue Room in 1991.

•

John Willoughby writes about food, health, and travel from his home in Cambridge, Massachusetts.

John grew up in rural Iowa, directly across the road from a traditional working farm. After graduating from Harvard University in 1970, he spent seventeen years working in various human-services positions. During this time, he also worked part-time for two years in the kitchen of the East Coast Grill. In 1989, Willoughby became a full-time writer, joining the staff of *Cook's* magazine as Feature Writer. He has continued to travel widely in Europe, northern Africa, the Near East, India, South America, and the Caribbean in search of new flavors and cuisines.

John is a regular contributor to *Metropolitan Home, Self, Eating Well,* and *Boston Magazine,* and his work has appeared in *GQ, The New York Times,* and various major metropolitan newspapers. He also served as Senior Consulting Writer for the Harvard AIDS Institute during its sponsorship of the International Conference on AIDS in 1992.